SONG
OF A
WATER DRAGON

SONG
OF A
WATER
DRAGON

by
Norman S. Track

YMAA Publication Center
Jamaica Plain, Mass. USA

Track, Norman S.
    Song of a water dragon / Norman S. Track.
    p. cm.
    Includes bibliographical references.
    Preassigned LCCN: 95-61879.
    ISBN: 1-886969-27-2.

    1. He, Yi An,–1908-1993. 2. China–History–20th century. 3.
Taoism–Biography. I. Title.

DS774.T73 1996   951
                                   QBI95-20668

First Printing 1996

2

Printed in Canada

YMAA

Publication Center

38 Hyde Park Ave., Jamaica Plain, MA 02130
1-800-669-8892

e-mail: **YMAA@aol.com**
home page: **http://infinite.org/ymaa**

CONTENTS

■ ACKNOWLEDGEMENTS

The author thanks He Yi An and his family, Hsuen Hai Tao, Hsuen Ke, Hsuen Shao Wen, Hsuen Song Tao, Lu Feng (all in Lijiang), Tim Comrie, Ellen Eisenberg, Kathleen Iacobacci, Barbara McConnell, Andrew Murray, Helen Rees, David Ripianzi, Frauke Voss, Edie Yolles, Hiromi Kobayashi, and Li Zeng.

水龍吟

THE ELUSIVE
WATER DRAGON

I first saw He Yi An in his handicrafts shop in the corner of the old market square. What a remarkable face. So distinctive. It conveyed wisdom and serenity. He saw me approach. From my closer vantage point, I sensed something special about him. Speaking neither Chinese nor Naxi, I beckoned him with hand gestures out of his shop into the natural light so that I might photograph him. Afterwards as I walked through the narrow lanes of Da Yan, I felt that this serendipitous meeting was the beginning of something. Of what I did not know.

One of my passions is to search for and document endangered species, both people and plants. Having photographed irises in their native habitats in Japan (1985) and Israel (1986), during the spring of 1987, I was in Lijiang, in the southwestern Chinese province of Yunnan, collecting information for a Chinese iris project. I was fortunate to be there because Lijiang County, an area rich in irises, had just opened to foreigners in 1985. During my first trip to China in December of that year, in the cities of Shanghai, Beijing, and Kunming, I had seen exclusively what I considered to be "Chinese" people. Now in Lijiang, in the countryside, for the first time I encountered minority nationalities, Chinese not of Han origin. The Naxi were one of these fifty-five other nationalities; it is thought that they migrated south from Tibet over one thousand years ago. Lijiang County was inhabited predominantly by the Naxi; in addition, there were significant numbers of Bai, Tibetan, Yi, and Han Chinese nationalities.

The minority nationalities were thoroughly fascinating. Many of them had royal families. The Clan Mu, the local Naxi royal family, practiced a number of religions. Many of their religious beliefs and practices were followed by their subjects. The Naxi brought their own *dongba* religion with them to Lijiang. It contains elements of Tibetan Bon. Most educated townspeople looked down upon the practice of the *dongba* as witchcraft. However, villagers believed that sickness was caused by evil spirits and frequently invited *dongba* to perform a ceremony to drive away the evil spirits.

The Clan Mu practiced a number of religions and considered building temples, or prayer rooms, to be good deeds. There were two large Buddhist Temples in Da Yan, and many smaller one-room buildings scattered among the villages. During the middle years of the Ming Dynasty (ca. 1500), the Clan Mu invited several Daoist families from Nanjing to Da Yan. Since many townspeople believed in Daoism, these priests were invited frequently to perform a number of ceremonies. The Clan Mu encouraged a group of wealthy men to join them in forming a *Dongjing*, or Daoist bible, Society. They met socially and for regular ritual gatherings. The common townspeople, interested in Daoism, belonged to the Huangjing Society. In the mountains outside of Lijiang, there were five lamaseries of the Karmapa (Red) Sect of Tibetan Lamaism. Most of the four hundred monks were Naxi from remote mountain areas; they were the children of poor families who could not afford to raise them. The remainder were from Tibet. There were several missionaries and a church in Da Yan; some Naxi children, but no adults, went to the church.

I discovered that two foreigners, Joseph Rock and Peter Goullart, had written about the Naxi and Lijiang. Joseph Rock, an Austrian-born American, came initially as a plant collector; subsequently, he explored the geography of the region and documented Naxi religious ceremonies and the *dongba* culture.[1]

Rock lived in a small village. He preferred to remain alone and generally did not socialize, with the Naxi. In contrast, Peter Goullart, a white Russian, was very much involved in the daily life of the Naxi as a Guomindang civil servant in the cooperative movement. The Guomindang was the amalgamation of rebellious elements that overthrew the Manchu dynasty and established the Republic of China in 1912. Goullart's *Forgotten Kingdom*[2] details his experience in Lijiang.

Pursuing my iris interests during the next two months, I first went to northeastern China and traveled in Manchuria and Inner Mongolia and then returned to Yunnan and traveled north of Lijiang. Through this effort I found nine irises in their native habitats and photographed them.

The following spring, I had the good fortune to be in Lijiang during the Sanduo (the Naxi god) Festival. At the Jade Dragon Park, an older Naxi man was singing and leading a circle folk dance. Later, another older Naxi, playing a reed pipe, led another folk dance. In one of the pavilions, a group of older Naxi men were performing *Dongjing*, Daoist bible, music. After entering the pavilion, I glanced at the orchestra. There he was! My eyes fixed on the old man from the market. He Yi An, looking very serious, was playing the ten gongs.

As he played the gongs and chanted, he was clearly in another world. Closing my eyes, I attempted to join him. "It was wonderful and extraordinary to hear the music which was played during the heyday of the glorious Han and Tang dynasties and, probably during the time of Confucius himself.... Their happiness was great and they did their best to express it in the elegant and classical manner of their ancestors who had drunk deeply of Confucian idealism. The old Sage had always taught that music was the greatest attainment of a civilized man; and to music they turned to express the exquisite joy of living and to enhance the serenity of their old age."[3]

Peter Goullart had been there half a century before.

The experience of this Sanduo Festival demonstrated the prominence of various types of music in Naxi culture. Since their music enchanted me, I decided to record Naxi folk and orchestral music. I organized to record *Dongjing* music by the Da Yan orchestra, a city group, and by the Bai Hua orchestra, a farmers group. One sunny Sunday afternoon, after recording *Dongjing* music in Bai Hua for several hours, I left for the Puji lamasery. A thirty minute bicycle trip and twenty minute walk up the mountain

Da Yan City Orchestra, March 1988.

brought me to Pujisi. The lamasery had been neglected for a long time but the courtyard was still a sanctuary. I sat on a stone step. The *Dongjing* music still filled my head. After a time, I started to walk slowly around the temple. About half way around, I paused for a moment and sat on a rock. I looked around the clearing and saw the elusive *Iris tectorum,* a rare iris species, looking back at me.

My fascination with the Naxi culture revealed through their music lured me back the following year to make further recordings. In the autumn of 1990, I recorded He Yi An chanting Daoist *sutras* in his two rooms. The color print that I had sent three years ago was hanging framed on the wall. That evening while listening to the recordings, I realized that He Yi An was one of the most important treasures of Lijiang, a living source of a rich cultural and spiritual tradition that seems to be nearing its end, given contemporary conditions and different life-styles. The thought of hearing more of his life, a life that encompassed often turbulent and changing times, excited me.

Fortunately, the previous year I had met Lu Feng, a local Han Chinese fluent in English and interested in journalism. The following morning with Lu Feng, I went to He Yi An's shop in the corner of the market and asked him if he would be interested in telling his life story. A smile came over his face as he replied, "I have been waiting for somebody to ask me to write down my life story."

From my many visits to Lijiang and my active interest in recording and learning about *Dongjing,* or Daoist bible music, I had developed a relationship, or as the Chinese would say a trust, with He Yi An. This trust made this project possible. I fully realized the problems inherent in attempting to write down his life story. I came from another time, another culture, another sensibility and spoke another language. Lu Feng became my Chinese mouth and ears.

We started our morning interviews with He Yi An in the courtyard behind his shop off the main market square. The second morning in response to a question, he replied, "The walls have ears." A former member of the Street Committee lived in the courtyard and he could not talk freely. He Yi An agreed to come to the Hsuen family courtyard where he talked, and sometimes chanted, at liberty.

As our interviews proceeded, I marveled at his intelligence and his incredible memory. When questioned about the *Da Dong Xian Jing*, the Daoist bible, he would often write the Chinese characters in the air as he talked. I could see him reliving the *Dongjing* gatherings as he described them. He portrayed fully his family religious and social festivals and detailed the family finances.

He Yi An's responses to my questions are presented in diary form with information from other family members and other sources as insights. The many social and religious activities are recorded in an Appendix.

This document of his life and times, *Song of a Water Dragon,* is folk anthropology. *Song of a Water Dragon* is also the title of an instrumental piece of *Dongjing* music. A water dragon is a Chinese symbol of dignity and power.

As the world moves rapidly towards a homogeneous culture, national boundaries and traditions come to mean less and less. Younger people throughout the world often have no idea of their cultural heritage. This is especially true in China. He Yi An's story provides a living testimony of how one man survived tremendous social, political, and economic changes. His life suggests that older traditions and religious beliefs may have survival advantage as part of their intrinsic worth.

Map of the Lijiang Area

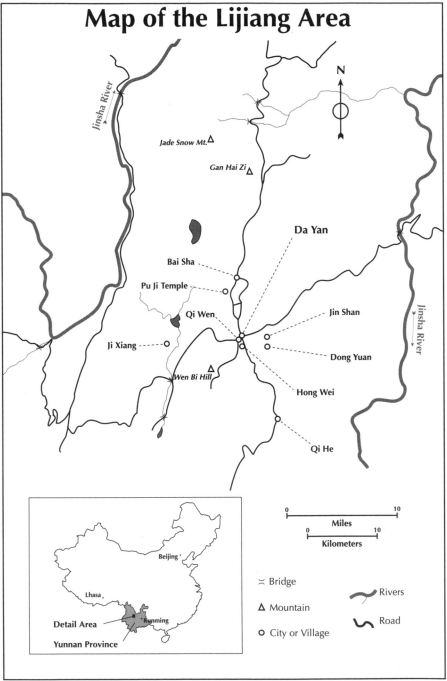

N

Jinsha River

Jade Snow Mt. △

Gan Hai Zi △

Da Yan

Bai Sha

Pu Ji Temple

Qi Wen

Jin Shan

Ji Xiang

Dong Yuan

Wen Bi Hill △

Hong Wei

Qi He

Jinsha River

| 0 | | | | | 10 |
Miles
| 0 | | | | | 10 |
Kilometers

Beijing

Lhasa

Kunming

Detail Area

Yunnan Province

)(Bridge

△ Mountain

O City or Village

Rivers

Road

FAMILY BACKGROUND

To understand my life, you must know something about my family background. Da Yan is a small town in the south-western Chinese province of Yunnan. In 1876, He Yang, my grandfather, completed his courtyard with twenty-four rooms in Qi Wen, a village within the town of Da Yan. The courtyard was filled with orchids, pine, bamboo, and plum trees. The upstairs rooms were decorated with calligraphy works, Chinese-style paintings, antiques, and bronze housewares. One of the rooms upstairs was a family chapel for *sutra* recitation. On a long table were three copper statues: Xuan Tian (a Daoist high priest), Guan Yin (the goddess of fertility and mercy), and Wen Chang (the god of literature), positioned from left to right.

Each morning after getting up, He Yang washed with fragrant water and dressed in clean clothes. Around seven o'clock, he entered the chapel, lit an oil lamp, and burned *joss* sticks. After exchanging pure water, he stood facing north and made a tea water and food offering; then, he placed his offerings on the table before the gods. After kneeling down and nodding his head three times, he sat in a chair facing north, breathed quietly, closed his eyes, and started to recite *sutras*[4] in a loud voice while beating a wooden fish[5]

If a great mind is blindfolded by countless desires[6]
It is only one inch wide

It flies south and north
It cannot tell west and east apart
Actually the mind is not covered with dust
It is not full of dreams and bitter desires
One should cherish his mind
One should choose only the Dao as his life's belief
If you let your mind be free and quiet, you should immediately
concentrate your desires
Thus paradise will be only one foot away from your mind

In his mind, he thought about the *sutra*, pronounced it correctly, and stood respectfully beside Wen Chang.

He Yang was an honest person who never touched liquor, or poppy, and was a scholar who passed the Imperial Examination at the county level. As a young man, He Yang had joined the *Dongjing* Society, a society for the local upper class. After learning the *Da Dong Xian Jing*, He Yang became a practicing Daoist. Society members believed that by doing some charity and some welfare they would achieve longevity and enjoy good fortune. They learned classics, rites, manners, music, and how to cultivate their personal character. Good at calligraphy, he often copied *sutras* and music notations. Being an only son, He Yang thought the Jade Emperor and Wen Chang would bless him with heirs if he practiced Daoism and cultivated his mind and character. He Yang with his wife, Sang Ma Ji, had two daughters and one son, He Ru Lin — my father.

After the Muslim uprising (1856-1874), He Zhao Lin, He Yang's father, had traveled to Lhasa with a caravan because the business opportunities were much better than in Da Yan. In Lhasa, he established a fur and leather handicrafts business. Since the business was so prosperous, in 1898, He Yang took his first son-in-law and a young relative to Lhasa to join his father's business. Shortly after they arrived in Lhasa, He Zhao Lin died. He Yang had to stay to run the family business. Sang Ma Ji had to remain in Da Yan to take care of their son and family. He Yang maintained a good relationship with his wife; she missed him very much. He sent her treasures, very precious red coral.

From Lhasa, He Yang supported his family by sending carpets and lamb skins to be sold in Da Yan. For a man of his position, it was common to have a female servant to cook, to wash his clothes and to take care of him. He Yang fell in love with Qi Li Du Ma, a Tibetan, and they married.

He Ru Lin, his son, had ten years of private schooling; he was very well educated. He stayed at home and learned the handicrafts business from his father. He Ru Lin was a master with apprentices in his shop. He visited his father three times in Lhasa. It was a difficult three-month journey. In some places there was no water, so they had to carry it for long distances. Some mountains took three days to ascend and another three days to descend.

In April, four or five families organized a caravan with twenty people and one hundred horses. They departed in May and each day a different family would lead the caravan; only the old horses knew the route. A large quantity of dried rice powder was taken from Da Yan. At specific intervals on their outward journey, leather bags, containing the dried rice powder, were hung on trees. Three months later, this food sustained them on their homeward journey. Because He Ru Lin was a kind man, he sometimes walked and let a servant ride his horse. When they stopped at a village, they sent a piece of white silk to the leader to pay their respects and assure safe passage.[7] Sugar candy, tea bricks, and silk were carried to Lhasa; lamb skins, Tibetan carpets, and wool to Da Yan.

He Ru Lin had a good singing voice and played several traditional Chinese instruments. Often with members of the *Dongjing* Society, He Ru Lin used his Daoist knowledge and musical talents to explain "profound mysteries" of some *sutras* or musical tunes.

When He Ru Lin was nineteen years old, he married Niu Fu Niang, a Naxi who could neither read nor write. At this time, it was quite common for girls to have no education. It was an arranged marriage. During the first seventeen years of their marriage, Niu did not give birth. So, when He Ru Lin was thirty-seven years old, he married Huang Qi Zhen, a twenty-seven year old Han woman, from Wei Xi County (about one hundred and fifty kilometers from Da Yan). Her father was a general and disliked common people; he had requested his daughter to wait for a husband from a wealthy family. When she came to Da Yan, a maid accompanied her, she continued to wear her Han clothing, and, because Naxi women worked, she stopped binding her feet.

After the second wedding, Niu Fu Niang remained in the same courtyard but lived and ate alone. She became a Buddhist; this was a common practice for women who could not give birth. Since she could not read, she went to a Buddhist temple where a monk taught her to recite *sutras*.

He Ru Lin forbade her to recite *sutras* in the family chapel. So, Niu Fu Niang prayed to Guan Yin at the temple. She was very sincere about her religious activities. She belonged to one of the groups of women who went to the temple to recite *sutras* on the first and fifteenth days of each month. Afterwards, they prepared a meal and ate together. Major gatherings for Guan Yin were held three times a year: on February 19th,[8] to celebrate her birthday; on June 19th, to commemorate the day she left home to become a Buddhist; and on September 19th, to honor the day she became immortal.

When Qi Zhen became pregnant, He Ru Lin went to the Wen Chang Temple and performed the Rite of Lighting a Candle and Making a Wish (See Appendix p. 124). Members performed this rite, before or after lunch, during the third ceremonial day of a *Dongjing* Society gathering. For the rite, He Ru Lin took a plate of rice and a string of fifty copper coins, two boxes of sugar, paper money, *joss* sticks, and a pair of candles to the temple. He gave these items to the family who took care of the temple. Before the ceremony, at a table outside the temple, a member, skilled in calligraphy, wrote the wishes in red ink on a piece of yellow paper. He Ru Lin wished for a son to continue the family; in addition, he promised to make him a student of Wen Chang and a member of the *Dongjing* Society.

The family economic condition was good. He Ru Lin and Qi Zhen worked together making leather clothing. Mandarin jackets sold for three silver dollars, coats (with sleeves) for nine, and long gowns for twenty. Their customers were mainly caravan men from Tibet, Dali, Baoshan, and Tengchong. Local wealthy people purchased coats and long gowns.

He Ru Lin had three apprentices training with him. They were thirteen to fourteen years old and came from either local or countryside families. The apprentices sent him a plate of rice, five hundred grams of tea and two boxes of red sugar and went down on their knees to acknowledge him as their master before studying with him. They lived in He Ru Lin's family courtyard and each day helped with the housework, cooking, cleaning, and fetching water. Once a month, He Ru Lin gave them pocket money; once a year, he gave them new clothes. After three years, they became masters themselves and then had to work for their master without wages for a year. After this year, they would be paid according to their productivity. During the winter months when He Ru Lin received new leather, he invited two masters to work with him for six months to help smooth and soften the leather.

Each year, the leather clothing business generated a profit of nine hundred to one thousand silver dollars. There was no income tax. An additional one hundred silver dollars came from their tenants selling the harvest from the family agricultural properties. The eight *mu* of land (approximately 1.3 acres), purchased by his great-grandfather and grandfather, was an average holding for a middle class family. The land rent income fluctuated depending upon the harvest. The government levied a land tax of less than one silver dollar. Townspeople and farmers paid similar taxes; although, most farmers, as tenants, paid rent to their landlords and no taxes.

He Ru Lin's prayer for a son was fulfilled with my birth in 1908. My father, or *baba* as Chinese boys call their fathers, was true to his word. He raised me to follow Wen Chang, and brought me into the *Dongjing* Society.

HIS STORY

1 9 0 8

My birth, on June 7th, fulfilled *Baba's* wish. He was so delighted that he invited many friends and relatives to a banquet.

In July, I became sick with convulsions; my parents treated me by placing pieces of ginger on the center and sides of my forehead and then heated the ginger. I responded to this ginger treatment and recovered. Because I had been sick, no "one-month-old" ceremony was held; *Baba* named me Jie Xian.[9]

1 9 0 9

Baba performed the Rite of Lighting a Candle and Making a Wish on three occasions for me at *Dongjing* Society gatherings. The first time was in February. Before lunch, Mama brought me to the temple; Niu Fu Niang, my stepmother, and several cousins also attended. *Baba* thanked Wen Chang for sending him a son and wished that Wen Chang would bless me with good health and good luck in the future.

When I was one year old, I was sick again with convulsions. At this time in Da Yan, Chinese herbal doctors were the only medical care available. *Baba* invited one of these doctors to examine me; the doctor could not make a diagnosis. He then invited a *dongba* to perform a ceremony for driving away evil ghosts. The *dongba* appeared in his ceremonial attire carrying a sword. The *dongba* burnt *joss* sticks and recited incantations. At the end of the ceremony, he threw a bowl of rice, soaked in cold water, outside the front gate. This gesture was to satiate the appetite of the evil ghosts so that they would not enter the house. As my condition remained unchanged, my father resorted to inviting a fortune teller.

After considering my five elements (metal, wood, water, fire, and earth), he stated that I lacked gold and other metals. Therefore, my name was changed to Jin Xuang, *jin* meaning gold. Again, my condition remained unchanged. Finally, Mama thought to try ginseng; it was expensive and believed to prolong life. After several months of ginseng treatment, I recovered. After my recovery, my family reverted to calling me Jie Xian.

1 9 1 0

When I was two years old, I listened to *Baba* recite *sutras* in the family chapel. He explained that he was reciting the *sutras* for me so that Wen Chang would protect me, give me good health, and guide me.

He Yang, my grandfather, died in Lhasa; his son-in-law held a funeral ceremony in Lhasa. When the news of my grandfather's death reached Da Yan six months later, *Baba* prepared a paper board describing his father. The family wore long, white gowns and held a ceremony in the main room downstairs. In the presence of the family, relatives, and friends, *Baba* lit *joss* sticks, made an offering and bowed down before the paper board. Following the common local tradition, seven days later *Baba* invited four Buddhist monks to hold a ceremony. The four monks recited *Bao Xiao Jing. (The Sutra of the Heart of Prajna, a sutra for rewarding parents)*. After this ceremony, the paper board was burnt.

1 9 1 1[10]

My stepmother lived in her own room in the same courtyard and cooked her own meals. *Baba* often quarreled with her and most of the time did not speak to her; Mama and my stepmother sometimes spoke, but did not have a good relationship. They quarreled over petty things. With the constant quarreling, I sometimes cried because I was so upset and frightened by the shouting. I asked them not to quarrel. My parents claimed that if my stepmother had a good attitude, then they could have a better relationship.

I spoke with my stepmother frequently. She spoke kindly to me and gave me sweets; as I was the only son, later she would have to depend upon me to take care of her. She went out most days and helped another family to mend caps. When I was young, she carried me on her back to the family graveyard for the Qing Ming Festival, a festival to pay respect to one's ancestors. (See Appendix p. 125).

My family graveyard was established during the Ming Dynasty (1368–1644 A.D.). The site was selected by a geomancer.[11] Facing the tombs, on the left the hills had the shape of a green dragon, on the right that of a white tiger; both were for protection. On the back, there was a mountain which represented treasure. In front of the graveyard, there was a flat hill which represented an offering table.

My parents told me that the Festival of Accepting and Sending Back Ancestral Spirits (See Appendix p. 126) was very important for our family. By inviting the souls of our ancestors to spend the festival with us, we demonstrated proper respect and gratitude to our ancestors. Also, our ancestors' spirits enjoyed a good meal with the family.

As a young boy, I was a dutiful son always showing filial obedience to my parents, and they treated me as a pet. Mama and grandmother took care of me. In the morning, grandmother woke me around ten o'clock. Some days, *Baba* slept this late. After washing, I dressed in a long gown, mandarin jacket, and six-pointed hat. Mama, or grandmother, served me a breakfast of *baba*, a Naxi bread, and Tibetan tea; sometimes I was served porridge. I ate in the courtyard corridor. Some mornings, my friends came over and we played in the courtyard; other mornings, I played in one of my friends' courtyards. Some mornings,

The family graveyard. Site of the Festival of Accepting and Sending Back Ancestral Spirits.

we went to the Qi Wen primary school, sat in the classroom, and listened to the lessons.

For lunch, the whole family ate rice, fried potatoes, and another vegetable. Following the local custom, on the second and sixteenth days of the month, a dish of salted meat was served. Fresh meat was served at festivals and gatherings. Twice a week, grandmother took me out for lunch to eat noodles at a small restaurant. This was a special treat because only wealthy people could afford to eat in restaurants. A bowl of noodles cost seven copper coins.

She reminisced about their house and life before the Muslim uprising (1856-1874). Before the Muslims defeated the local army, the citizens of Da Yan escaped to the outlying villages and other counties. The Muslims occupied Da Yan and burnt all the houses. She told me how hard my grandfather had worked to provide the money to build the house we lived in.

Because of the difficult economic times, many Naxi ceremonies were simplified, such as weddings and funerals, or even disappeared after the uprising because people could not afford the expenditure. For example, among the common people a wedding couple had to borrow clean clothes for their ceremony.

Life now was better than before the uprising. Each day, grandmother gave me three or four copper coins[12] as pocket money; I used this pocket money to buy sweets and candies. In the afternoon, I played with my friends.

The whole family gathered for supper at six o'clock. During the evenings under the light of a plant oil lamp, *Baba* taught me to read and write Chinese and calligraphy as my pre-school education. Mama taught me to speak Chinese. She was from a good

Han family; she was quiet, calm, and cautious. She treated me well.

Baba's friends in the *Dongjing* Society often came drinking, talking, smoking poppy by turns, playing music, singing, or chanting poems. Our family enjoyed a happy, trouble-free, care-free life. As a boy, I always looked forward to the excitement of New Year's Eve and Spring Festival, the Chinese New Year. (See Appendix p. 127-132). Many things were purchased for Spring Festival because most of the shops were closed for fifteen days.

1 9 1 5

During the February *Dongjing* Society gathering at the Wen Chang Temple, *Baba* performed the Rite of Lighting a Candle and Making a Wish to celebrate my "growing up" ceremony. I was about to start primary school. He was proud of me and wanted to take good care of me.

At this gathering, I would become a member of the *Dongjing* Society. I would learn good manners. I would become a gentleman. This was my first visit, as an adult, to the Wen Chang Temple. In preparation, my head was shaven, I had a bath in cypress leaf scented water, and dressed in new clothes. I wore a long, dark green gown, a black mandarin jacket, and a black silk, six cornered hat with a central red ball. All members wore black mandarin jackets for the gatherings. I had a sense that I was growing up and becoming an adult. I was very proud and happy that I could wear new clothes and that I had a higher social position than others. *Baba* told me to behave respectfully in the temple and not to look directly at the statue of Wen Chang.

Baba wished that Wen Chang would bless me, that I would be intelligent, successful in my studies, and would become somebody important in life. Since I had lived seven years, I was considered an adult; many children died of measles at two to three years of age. At this ceremony, I was given a school name: Zhi Qiang. *Baba* wrote my name in the *Yong Bao Ping An,* or *Safety Forever,* a book containing all of the current members of the *Dongjing* Society. By putting my name in the book *Baba* made me a member. After the ceremony, I met many members, *Baba*'s friends; they greeted me warmly and encouraged me to study hard and become a good member of the *Dongjing* Society. They admired me.

That evening at home, grandmother cooked me a table of vegetarian dishes to congratulate me on becoming a member of the *Dongjing* Society. *Baba* then started to teach me *sutras,* music, and musical instruments during the evenings and on Sundays. *Baba* told me the story of Wen Chang from the *Da Dong Xian Jing.*

文昌大洞仙經序

九天開化司祿宏仁帝君撰并玄契贊

予生吳會居事畎會忽於鋤下得一金像詞

之父老曰乃元始天王像昔夏禹理水合金

為像以鎮方域予香火奉祀未嘗少關因海

風翻浪人力不能支丁為眾捨金像投駭浪

Chinese characters from the Wen Chang story.

I was born in the State of Wu. I was a farmer. One day while I was hoeing in the field, I found a gold statue in the soil. I returned home and showed it to some old men in the village. They said, "It is the statue of Yuan Shi Tian Wang (the Primordial Heaven King). Long ago when Xia Yu brought a large flood under control, he molded the gold statue for guarding this area." Thus, daily I started to make sacrifices to the statue with profound respect. I burnt *joss* sticks, made food offerings and bowed.

Once the lake became terribly rough and caused great damage to the people. All the village areas near the lake were threatened with great danger. I threw the gold statue into the lake. As the rough waters subsided, the lake gradually became calm and the whole area became safe. After this event, frequently I missed the statue. One day at dusk, as I took my walk by the lake, suddenly I saw a mound of sand giving out a beautiful light. The sky became bright. I went to the mound and dug out the gold statue. I took the statue home. All the villagers helped me to construct a temple for the statue. We made sacrifices to the statue for many years and it became more and more magical.

Because the statue was very efficient, we received more and more rewards.

One year, my wife suddenly died of cholera. The day when I was building her tomb, three immortals visited me. Their clothing was like colorful bird feathers, their caps were made of hemp cloth. They wore straw shoes and each of them held a bamboo stick in their hand. They gave me a volume of the *Da Dong Xian*

Jing and told me that if I recited the *sutras* at dawn and at dusk I surely would receive good rewards. They claimed that reciting the *sutras* would provided three benefits.

"The first benefit is that you can help the souls of your parents and forefathers to leave hell. The second benefit is that you can drive out crime and disasters and achieve longevity and good fortune. The third benefit is that you can save other's lives. If you make sacrifices to the statue and study with us, we shall inscribe your name on the list of Heaven."

On the right day, I listened to them and prepared a vegetable offering to sacrifice to the gold statue and accepted them as my teachers. Since that day, without interruption, I have studied the and daily recited the *Da Dong Xian Jing sutras* at dawn and dusk. From these activities, I developed the ability to prophesy.

During a hot summer, there was a flood and the water surrounded my wife's tomb. I made a sacrifice to the gold statue and recited the *sutras* a thousand times and, at last, the tomb was safe. In the autumn of the following year, it rained heavily for several weeks. Brooks near the tomb became turbulent rivers. I worried about my wife's tomb. When the rain became a drizzle, I went to the tomb and, to my surprise, the graveyard had become a small hill about one kilometer square. The tomb was in quite good condition.

My parents died of cholera. I missed them often and detested the cholera ghosts. Since it was impossible to find the way to hell, I could not take revenge upon them. So, I studied the *sutras* diligently. I prayed that the gold statue would give me the strength to subdue the cholera ghosts. Three years passed. One night in a dream, the gold statue spoke to me, "You are quite familiar with the *Da Dong Xian Jing*; however, you have not seen the *Da Dong Fa Lu*. Now, I shall teach you how to use the incantations to drive out evil ghosts. Afterwards, you can fulfill your wish and take revenge upon the cholera ghosts. You can play the role of helping the immortals and you can support your country and help people."

The gold statue took two books out of his sleeve. Repeatedly, I bowed and thanked the gold statue. When I awoke, two incantations books were on my pillow. I held a ceremony to express my thanks to the gold statue and later purchased a delicate wooden box in which to store the books. Only on lucky days, I took the books out and read them.

One day while reading, I came to a sentence; "Ask Heaven to send ten thousand persons to earth." Suddenly there was a strong wind and thunder. Through the mist, countless people appeared wearing suits of golden armor and red helmets. First, they stood in front of me; then, they knelt down and asked me for an order. One person, holding a small red flag, standing in front of the others, said, "We shall obey your order." I was almost in a trance. I shouted loudly, "I want you to drive out the cholera ghosts from Zhang Bo Yuan's family, one of my neighbors in this village. All the family have cholera. Go and drive out the cholera!"

After I said this, the person who held the red flag led a hundred persons into Zhang Bo Yuan's house. Minutes later, they drove out five ghosts. One wore a tiger's skin, one had a head like a cock, one had a body like a man, one had a head like a raven, and one had a head like a donkey. The first ghost held water, the second fire, the third feathers, the fourth an ax, and the fifth a chisel. I felt quite angry and gave the order to destroy them.

One of the ghosts said, "My name is Zhang Bo Yuan. My four friends and I have come from hell. We were created by nature and, therefore, cannot be destroyed. Although we have our own tasks, we only travel to where we are told to go. Those persons on earth who get sick or die, it is their fate. It is not our decision to make them sick or kill them. The officials in hell report a person's earthly deeds to the Jade Emperor in Heaven. These officials suggest a punishment. If the Jade Emperor agrees with their suggestion, the officials decide the type of punishment to be distributed to the person, either illness or death. We visit the person's home and carry out the officials' orders. We never thought that we would meet a real immortal today. If you forgive us, afterwards, we shall obey you and listen to you. When we are spreading cholera to some persons if we see your incantations on their gates, we shall not enter that home and make the persons sick."

I taught the persons that had cholera in the area the magical arts according to the incantation books, and they recovered. I cured countless patients and my fame spread far and wide. Swarms of poor people and rich officials came to my home. My knowledge and good behavior resulted from my study and understanding of the *Da Dong Xian Jing*; but the *Da Dong Fa Lu* gave me the magical ability to uphold justice and oppose evil, help the living, expiate the sins of the dead, avoid disasters, and obtain longevity. Later good ghosts and spirits often came in the mist, or from the nether world, and asked me to recite *sutras* for them. If I recited *sutras* for them, they thanked me and said, "After listening to your *sutra* recitation, our magical ability has developed and we now have the capacity to do more good deeds."

The souls of those who had drowned came to me while I was in a dream and invited me to recite *sutras* so that their floating souls could land on earth. After I recited *sutras* for them, they thanked me and said, "Because of your *sutra* reciting, our souls left the misery and obtained new lives."

In one bad year diseases spread seriously. Many people became sick. I recited *sutras* and used the incantation books to call the soldiers from Heaven. These soldiers came to earth and caught the cholera ghosts and bad devils dispensing poison and ruining food. Many good spirits helped the soldiers take control over the diseases. After this, we informed Heaven about the bad year and diseases on earth. The gods in Heaven told the spirits in charge of the ghosts in hell and the spirits in charge of land and mountain to help us to cure the diseases. Those spirits who did not come to help when they heard my reciting of *sutras* and incantations would be punished.

The Dao is full of mercy. God is kind-hearted. God likes to save people and forbids killing. Those persons who master the incantation books must not use the magical arts to harm others. If they do so, God surely will punish them.

Those who want to master the magical arts must sacrifice to the *sutra* and incantation books. From this activity they will receive rewards. They must do things properly. Those who want to learn the incantation book must study the book diligently. The benefits of the incantation books are that they can help you to make friends, reduce hatred, protect your house and tombs, pray for a good harvest, avoid animals, avoid illness, protect your friends and relatives, cease battles, have good fortune, avoid flood and drought, kill bad ghosts, help the souls of your forefathers to leave hell, and protect your village and country. All those desires will come true if you sacrifice to the gold statue, the *sutra* and incantation books. Those who believe in the Dao should visit and study with real Daoist masters. Thus their ability will become stronger and they will gradually understand the profound meaning of the Dao.

Actually, it was through reciting *sutras* that I won my reputation and respect. I became a god in Heaven and can live forever. God is sensitive and knows everything. To those who have the *sutras*, if you recite them diligently, surely you will have a good reward.

I hope someday when I return to Heaven I shall be with all the members of the *Dongjing* Society.

I kept the story of Wen Chang in my mind and thought about it often.

During February, I started to attend the Qi Wen primary school.[13]

The boys were from farmers', tailors', cobblers', or handicraftsmen's families. Parents encouraged girls to go to school. Most girls were shy so the Lijiang County Education Bureau set up a separate school; some girls from wealthy, or traditionally intellectual families studied with private tutors at home.

My school courses were Chinese language, mathematics, and calligraphy. For the first two years, we studied the *Three Characters Classic, One Thousand Character Primer,* and *One Hundred Family Name Primer.* We were taught to pronounce the characters and to memorize them; no explanation, no understanding. During the second two years, a new Chinese language textbook was introduced with pictures to demonstrate the meaning of the characters. We started to understand the meaning of the characters.

I got up before the sun rose and had breakfast of *baba* and Tibetan tea. School started at eight o'clock; there were three lessons until noon. I went home for lunch; Mama usually prepared rice, fried potatoes, and another vegetable. I returned to school for another three lessons from two until five o'clock. The supper menu was the same as at lunchtime.

I was excited when my father took me to my first *Dongjing* gathering, May 13th. When I entered the temple, I felt that I had entered another world. Members showed respect to the gods and to one another. Everybody spoke softly. I sensed that the temple was a holy place. I enjoyed the opportunity during the meals to socialize with the members, both old and young. My father had instructed me how to kneel down to show my respect to the older members during the gathering.

From this very meaningful and special experience, I decided to study diligently the *sutras* and the music.

I thought that because my father had performed the Rite of Lighting a Candle and Making a Wish I had came to this earth. Wen Chang had rewarded my father by fulfilling his wish for a son. I became more interested in learning about the Dao. I envied the older members of the *Dongjing* Society because they knew everything about the *sutras* and the music. Because of my keen interest, older members instructed me how to recite the *sutras* and play the instruments.

My teacher knew that I had a good family background so he agreed when my father asked if I could have leave to attend the *Dongjing* Society gatherings. Afterwards, my classmates envied me and asked me what we ate at the gatherings and how much of the *sutras* I remembered. Their questions encouraged and

Moo Show Shen – Musical Notation.

stimulated me to learn more; I was proud to be a member of the *Dongjing* Society.

My father taught me more than I learned at primary school. He told me even if I did not learn other things at school, I would understand life through the *Da Dong Xian Jing*, the Daoist *sutras*. I felt that my school was not important. My father took me to the *Dongjing* Society gatherings. I knew many of the members because they were my father's friends and visited our house. When I met them in the street, I showed them proper respect by bowing. I behaved more politely and with a better manner than other boys my age.

The happiest times in my childhood were participating in the *Dongjing* Society, visiting the Wen Chang Temple, learning *sutras* and musical instruments. Sometimes I even skipped my classes to study *sutras* or practice music.

Because of all the time I spent on the *Dongjing* Society activities, I was ashamed that I could not keep up with the other students in mathematics. Sometimes the teacher scolded me for skipping classes. However, in his notebook, the teacher recorded a good judgment on my page because I was well behaved and generally a good student.

Primary school education took four years; most boys then went into society and continued their father's career as a handicraftsman or a businessman. Because I had missed so much school, the teacher told my father that I should study for a further year at primary school.

My family lived well in our large courtyard with four buildings; in addition to the substantial income from our leather clothing business, we were landlords receiving rent income from our eight *mu* of agricultural lands. Most other families labored to earn their way and lived in much smaller dwellings. I had as much pocket money as I wanted; only two of my ten friends had pocket money. My mother often invited my three poorer friends to join us for a good meal. I often bought things for my friends. They respected me for being from a wealthy family.

In March, before planting, there was a Dragon Fair in the park lasting over ten days. There was a daily performance of Peking Opera. The *Dongjing* Society played music during the fair. Flowers, handicrafts, and other commercial products were exhibited in tents. I was told that before 1911 on one day there had been a ceremony for the Dragon King. Both townspeople and farmers knelt in front of the Dragon King statue, lit *joss* sticks, and prayed. The townspeople prayed for a prosperous year; the farmers prayed for rain for their crops and a good harvest. Legends tell of immortal dragons who can change their shape into that of a man. The Dragon King statue, in the form of a man with long teeth, was an embodiment of a dragon. The dragon lived in the sea and was in charge of rain. No rain meant drought, a bad harvest. At the Dragon Fair, I sponsored my friends to sample different foods at the many restaurants in the park.

Young boys, ten years old, had bad habits, smoking poppy and gambling. These boys stole things from their homes and sold them to buy poppy. Some of my friends had these bad habits. I neither smoked poppy nor gambled.

1 9 1 6

Grandmother's death, in November, was the first time that I was really sad. On the day of her demise, the family wore long, white cloth gowns, erected a long pole in front of the gate and hung a long white paper with her birth and death dates written on it. The family informed relatives and friends;[14] close relatives were sent long, white cloth gowns which they wore during the three-day funeral ceremony. My father wore a bamboo hat with three pieces of bamboo sticking up from the rim, the sign of a dutiful first son; I wore a bamboo hat with one piece of bamboo sticking up, the sign of a dutiful first grandson. We both wore straw shoes. On all three days in the family chapel, Buddhist monks recited *sutras.* On the second day, the *Dongjing* Society held a ceremony in the evening, playing *Ten Offerings* and chanting the *Twenty-four Piety Sutras.*[15] On the third day, the coffin was carried out of the house. Immediate family and close relatives knelt down on the road by a stream while the coffin passed over them. The bamboo hats were thrown into the stream.

1 9 1 8

When I was 10 years old, I started to attend the Confucian gatherings with my father. (See Appendix p. 132).

1 9 2 0

I entered a higher primary school in Da Yan which provided a more comprehensive education.[16] The twenty teachers taught mathematics, history, geography, Chinese language and composition, and morality. The whole school had four classes; each class had about sixty students. There were no girl students. Most students went to higher primary school because of their parents; they were really not interested in their studies. I was like the other students. Similar to primary school, I obtained permission to miss classes to attend the *Dongjing* Society's activities. Sometimes I discussed the activities of the *Dongjing* Society with the other students; they were envious. Zhang Chun Xiao, a classmate, was also a member of the *Dongjing* Society; however, the activities did not interest him.

Each month, my father paid a deposit to a pub so that every morning I had a bowl of broth and two steamed grilled meat buns for my breakfast. Only boys from wealthy families could eat such a breakfast; the other boys, who ate bread or steamed buns, envied me.

When I was thirteen years old, I continued my schooling but did not think about a profession; my parents encouraged me to sit the university entrance examination. I obeyed my parents in everything. My parents told me that there was sufficient family money to maintain me so that I did not have to worry about my financial support. My father wanted me to be a local official or a middle school teacher.

1 9 2 1

My father wanted to travel to Lhasa to carry his father's bones back to Da Yan. Because of his business commitments, he was too busy to make the trip. Therefore, he wrote a letter to his uncle informing him that four families had organized two horses to transport their relatives' remains back to Da Yan. In January, my grandfather's bones reached Da Yan in a wooden box covered with an ox-leather bag. According to Naxi tradition it was bad luck to have bones of a deceased family member enter the house through the main gate; the box was carried into the courtyard through the shop entrance.

On that day, the family wore long, white cloth gowns, erected a long pole in front of the gate and hung a long white paper with his birth and death dates written on it. The family informed relatives and friends; close relatives were sent long, white cloth gowns which they wore during the seven day funeral ceremony. My father wore a bamboo hat with three pieces of bamboo sticking up from the rim; I wore a bamboo hat with one piece of bamboo sticking up. We both wore straw shoes. On all seven days in the family chapel, Buddhist monks recited *sutras*. On the second day, the *Dongjing* Society held a ceremony in the evening playing *Ten Offerings* and chanting the *Twenty-four Piety Sutras*. On the seventh day, the bones were transferred into a new coffin and it was carried out of the courtyard. The immediate family and close relatives knelt down on the road after a stream while the coffin passed over them. The bamboo hats were thrown into the stream. The coffin was carried to the family graveyard and buried next to grandmother, his wife.

By this time, I had mastered with sufficient proficiency the *sutras* and musical instruments to participate fully in the *Dongjing* Society orchestra. *Bagua* was the first piece that I played. Although I could not play perfectly, I was very excited to play in the orchestra. My father was very satisfied with my standard of performance; the older members admired me and realized my potential to become a prominent member of the Society in the years ahead. My keen interest in the flute led to a comprehensive understanding of Daoism because I first learned the *sutras* and then the music.

I saw my schoolmates who smoked poppy, gambled, and were in poor health. I did not want to be like them. At this time, I consciously decided to take Wen Chang as the model for my life.

Because knowledge and use of Chinese language were considered by many as the most important measure of an educated person, my parents wanted me to broaden my educational base. To accomplish this, they arranged for me to study at my uncle's private school for about a year and a half. My uncle was a well known scholar and poet. Each morning, his six students bowed down in front of him. We studied *The Four Books*, *The Five Classics*, *Primer and Precious Readings for Children,* and other Chinese classics. Often after the class, I stayed at my uncle's house, and my aunt cooked good dishes for me. My uncle spent extra time with me providing more extensive explanations of these Chinese classics. When I walked in the street with him, because he was so well known, people greeted both of us warmly and with great respect.

1 9 2 3

When I was fifteen years old, my father arranged for me to marry Zhao Yu Ji. As was custom at the time, I was informed only after my father had concluded the arrangement. Her family was in the fur business and did not own land. My family sent her clothing, gold earrings, and jade. Before the engagement, according to the ethical code of the time, we had seen each other but had not spoken. A young man spoke freely with women in his family, but it was considered bad manners to speak with women outside your family. The society centered around the men. Men and women were often entertained separately. On festivals, our families exchanged invitations for supper; because we were both quite shy, we avoided each other on these occasions.

In mid-February, a five day gathering was organized to celebrate Hua Jia Sheng Hui,[17] a sixty-year cycle celebration, an old Chinese tradition. All the local religious groups, Daoist, Lama, Buddhist, and *Dongba*, participated by reciting *sutras* to help the people have a good life and the country be prosperous. Some days they all celebrated together. On the third day, they held separate events; a senior Daoist priest organized a ceremony for accepting the gods.

The priest dressed as the Jade Emperor and selected thirty-six boys from good families to represent different gods (e.g. light, thunder, rain); each boy wore a Peking Opera general's uniform. I was Marshal Lu, the God of Protection. The son of the Clan Mu played the first god of the thirty-six.

The gods, divided into four groups, were positioned on the four sides of the park. To start the ceremony, the Jade Emperor stood on a high platform in the center and recited incantations calling the gods from heaven. The sound of firecrackers excited the two thousand spectators.

The Jade Emperor first summoned the gods from the east. The nine gods approached the Jade Emperor on horseback and inquired, "For what have you called us?"

"You must come tomorrow for a parade." replied the Jade Emperor. The Jade Emperor repeated this protocol with the other three groups of gods. Then, when the Jade Emperor called a god's name, that god appeared on horseback with a sword in his right hand. While riding around the central platform, each god recited loudly the *Incantation of Golden Lights* from the *sutra* book *Opening Prayer*.

The origin of all life comes from heaven and earth
I have been cultivating my body and mind
I shall experience countless disasters
I shall prove the greatness of the Dao
In the three worlds[18]
Only our Dao is lofty
If my body could give off a golden light
No one could hear nor see me
The great Dao could embrace heaven and earth
It has been bringing up all the things that have life
If I recite this incantation again and again
My body will give off golden light
Gods from the three worlds will escort me
The five gods[19] welcome me
Countless deities will bow to me
I shall make thunder my servant
When evil ghosts see me they will be scared to death
Bad spirits will disappear
I shall have thunderbolts
Gods of thunder will avoid me
The Dao has joined my life
I am full of vigor
Golden light please appear at once
Please appear and escort my body
Wen Chang bless me

Dressed as Marshal Lu participating in this ceremony in front of all these people I felt like a real god. After the Jade Emperor had accepted each of the gods, the ceremony ended.

The next morning at ten o'clock, there was a parade through the streets. The governor of Lijiang County led the parade followed by a large group of children. The thirty-six gods followed on horseback with members of the *Dongjing* Society orchestra walking behind them playing music. Lamas reciting *sutras* and beating gongs were next in the parade. Monks and *dongba* followed. Interspersed among the religious participants, others walked carrying lit *joss* sticks and lit off firecrackers. Spectators along the parade route arranged tables with burning *joss* sticks, fruit, candies, and tea water. Parade participants could stop for refreshment.

That year, I entered the Third Middle School of Yunnan Province.[20] The school had two hundred male students, with fifty per class. The upstairs rooms of the school building were dormitories. In the center of each dormitory was a wooden platform on which thirty boys slept. Behind each boy's head was an oil lamp so he could read in the evening. An older teacher was our supervisor and rang a bell to wake us at six o'clock in the morning. I dressed in a long blue gown, a black embroidered mandarin jacket, and a cap. Then we had our breakfast which consisted of porridge, steamed buns or *baba*. We either read books or exercised in the playing field until the first lesson at eight o'clock. On Wednesday and Saturday mornings, the first lesson was physical exercise; for this, we wore white cloth uniforms and white hats; we ran five kilometers. After the second lesson which finished at eleven o'clock, we had lunch. In the dining hall, eight students sat at table; we were served a pot of rice, a bowl of soup, and three bowls of vegetables. There was plenty of good quality food.

After lunch, we had free time; some rested, some read books; some went out of the school yard and smoked poppy and gambled. Others, including myself, participated in a calligraphy society. Each member contributed some money and each day we would write characters. If a student drew a wrong character, he had to pay a fine. The moneys collected were used to sponsor brush painting for the better students.

The four afternoon lessons were taught from one to five o'clock. For supper, we were served a pot of rice, a bowl of soup, one bowl of meat, and two bowls of vegetables. After supper, we had free time. Usually during this time, I read classical Chinese literature. Some evenings, the members of the calligraphy society handed their assignments to the older student leader. For those who had drawn a good character, he drew a red circle on their papers.

When it was getting dark, we returned to our classrooms where lit oil lamps had been placed on each desk. Two students sat at each desk as our teacher reviewed the material covered that day. At ten o'clock we returned to the dormitory. My roommates knew that I was a member of the *Dongjing* Society and could play the flute. Some evenings they asked me to play the flute before we went to sleep.

Life during the week in the dormitory was interesting. I talked with my classmates, read my books, played my flute, and sang songs. During primary school, my parents told me what to do and I obeyed; during middle school I felt freer, I had more knowledge, and my parents seldom controlled me. At home on the weekends, Mama cooked me good meals and I played with my friends.

My friend, Zhang Chun Xiao, did not attend middle school; his father, a prominent scholar, turned up his nose at the curriculum of the middle school. He believed that good composition was most important. So Zhang Chun Xiao attended his father's private school. My parents wanted me to go to Middle School; however, during vacations, they sent me to my uncle's private school for further classical education. Zhang Chun Xiao and I remained friends by spending time together on weekends.

1 9 2 6

In November, I married Yu Ji. (Wedding ceremonies and festivities described in Appendix p. 133). I was eighteen years old and a second grade student at middle school. She, four years my senior, could neither read nor write, which was common for women at that time. My classmates wrote the invitations with black inked characters on red paper and distributed them two days before the wedding to about one hundred and thirty guests. The wedding festivities lasted four days.

After my marriage, I continued to live at school and was at home on weekends. I was pleased with Yu Ji; she respected my

Yu Ji, his first wife.

parents, obeyed them, and they liked her. She cooked for the whole family including the three apprentices. I was very happy at this time.

According to Chinese custom, until a new wife has developed a relationship with her in-laws and is accepted fully as one of the family, she shows respect and good manners in their presence by not talking loudly and only when spoken to. When alone in the evening, we talked. We went to her family on the second day of Spring Festival. She took a plate with rice and two boxes of sugar as gifts. Upon arrival at her house, we went upstairs for a ceremony for ancestors in front of the wooden boards; we returned downstairs and knelt down in front of her parents. Then, we visited my uncle before returning home for lunch. Yu Ji and I also visited her parents in July during the Festival of Accepting and Sending Back Ancestral Spirits.

In December, a Kunming *qigong* master came to Da Yan and established a *Qigong* Society. For two months, I studied daily for two hours with the master. Only when your mind is calm and

He Yi An practicing *qigong.*

quiet can you practice *qigong*, the practice of which promotes good health by stimulating the five body parts, thereby driving away disease. Through *qigong* one achieves longevity.

I started to practice *qigong* while reciting my *sutras*.

> *The great Dao has given us life[21]*
> *We do qigong to build up the five deities[22]*
> *We wish we could subdue the terrible devils[23]*
> *Thus our minds will always be quiet and pure*
> *We must cut off our countless desires*
> *We must drive out the disasters*
> *Only when we subdue our desires*
> *Our behavior will be in keeping with the Dao*
> *Wen Chang bless me*

1 9 2 7

On May 13th, my father took me to the General Guan Temple accompanied by Yu Ji, Mama, and stepmother to perform the Rite of Lighting a Candle and Making a Wish to register my adult name, Yi An. My adult name had been selected by my teacher at middle school and my uncle. My adult name was written on the *Dongjing* Society record *Safety Forever.*

My first daughter was born in July. When she was born, I felt quite happy. In October, she died of convulsions. When she died, I was quite sad. There was no ceremony and she was buried on a wild hill. I did not want her bad spirits in the family graveyard.

My parents encouraged me to continue my education at Donglu University, in Kunming. Since I had a Middle School graduation certificate, I was eligible to sit the entrance examination. So, in November, Zhang Chun Xiao borrowed a cousin's certificate and we rented horses, joined seven caravan men from Qi Wen, and set out for the eighteen day journey to Kunming. On the third day out from Da Yan, around eleven o'clock in the morning, thirty robbers suddenly dashed out from the bushes carrying clubs, knives, and spears. Some wore leather jackets, others long gowns; all had painted their faces with black ink.

"Kill them! Kill them!", they shouted as they surrounded us. I was very frightened. I almost had a heart attack. Quickly, they searched us for money. In a short time, the robbers disappeared into the bushes with our money, luggage, and goods. Robberies often occurred along this road but we had hoped to be lucky and pass safely. I lost thirty silver dollars that were in my luggage; I still had ten silver dollars that the robbers did not find in their quick search of my clothing.

I was very nervous when I returned to Da Yan. Zhang Chun Xiao took some money from his father and wanted me to go with him to Kunming. My parents suggested that I try the examination the following year. I was still too frightened to leave Da Yan. Zhang Chun Xiao went to Kunming and sat the entrance examination in his cousin's name. He passed the examination, changed his enrolled name to his own, and attended Donglu University. He wrote encouraging me to sit the entrance examination the following year.

1 9 2 8

At this time, the headmaster of the Third Middle School was renting a room in my family's courtyard. The headmaster recommended that the Lijiang County Education Bureau arrange a job for me. Starting in March, I was the teacher at the Qi Wen primary school. My salary was fifteen silver dollars for a semester. There were thirty boys in my class. At the request of the boys' parents, I used *Three Characters Classic* and *One Hundred Family Name Primer* instead of the newer textbooks. Since my parents wanted me to sit the university entrance examination the following year, they thought that teaching would give me the opportunity to review my lessons.

I was pleased that I could still attend the *Dongjing* Society activities while another teacher substituted for me. Also, since I had had the privilege to study for so many years, I felt a responsibility to do something for others and teach young students.

Over the coming years, the family income fell to four hundred silver dollars plus a land rent income of one hundred silver dollars. The land tax remained just less than one silver dollar. Rice cost seven to eight copper coins per *jin*.

1 9 2 9

On June 29th, my father died of dysentery at the age of fifty-seven. The dysentery was caused by smoking new poppy; I hated poppy.

On the day of his demise, we set up a white tent and informed relatives and friends.[24] The memorial ceremony lasted twelve days. I wore a long white, cloth gown, a bamboo hat with three pieces of bamboo sticking up, and straw shoes for the twelve days. On the second day, the *Dongjing* Society held a ceremony in the evening, playing *Ten Offerings* and chanting the *Twenty-*

four Piety Sutras. For ten days, the family entertained visitors paying condolence calls. No Buddhists monks were invited because Mama told me that now we must manage our family finances economically. Mama and stepmother spoke to each other during the ten days of the funeral ceremony. On July 11th, my family invited ten porters to carry the coffin to the family graveyard.

My father's death saddened me greatly and I wanted to cry; but being a real man, I swallowed my tears.

I consulted a geomancer to select an appropriate position for my father's grave. I put a stone tablet on the tomb with my father's name leaving space for Mama's. Before the stone tablet, I knelt and prayed that Wen Chang bless me with a son, an heir. Each year on the anniversary of my father's demise, I ate vegetarian meals and made an offering to my father's memory.

My father's dying wishes were that I support the family, keep the family property, and treat Mama well. I behaved as a dutiful son and, after my father's demise, I built tombs for my ten ancestors. To do this, I spent several hundred silver dollars; this extravagance plus the four hundred silver dollars spent for the funeral affected the family business. After my father's death, since I was born in June, I became a host for the June *Dongjing* gathering. I enjoyed teaching, the social position it afforded me, and wanted to remain a teacher. People were told to pay respect in the following order: Heaven, Earth, Emperor, Minister, and Teacher. A teacher had a good reputation, better than a businessman.

However, Mama remarked to me "The dead cannot come alive, a family must continue its life and business."

Thus, as a dutiful son, I listened to Mama. I quit teaching, did not sit the university entrance examination, and entered the family fur and leather business.

I had learned handicrafts from my father but was not as skilled. However, my skills were sufficient for me to be regarded as a master; there were two apprentices in my shop and two masters joined us during the winter months. However, I seldom was present at work as I was always busy with my social activities. Besides the *Dongjing* Society activities, wealthy people were always inviting me to their homes; I believed that it was not socially correct to refuse them. In addition, I was very fond of music, socializing, and good food.

Because of my absence and my mother's inability to manage the business, the masters and apprentices seized the opportunity to take significant amounts of money. As well, Yu Ji was sending money and grain to support her family. Profits and capital declined dramatically each year. I was fully aware of the family financial situation. Even with the substantial loss of income, I felt that there were more than sufficient funds to support the family. Thus, I continued to direct my energy and interest into the *Dongjing* Society and my social life.

After I entered my family business, I began to attend the Fur and Leather Society gatherings (See Appendix p. 136). Sometimes the date of the Fur and Leather Society gathering conflicted with the Qing Ming Festival; I often went to my family graveyard in the morning and to the gathering in the afternoon.

My first son was born in July; after only seven days, he died. There was no ceremony and the body was buried on a wild hill. I was terribly sad to lose my first son.

1 9 3 0

My second daughter was born in February; she died of measles in August. I was quite sad to lose her.

1 9 3 2

Zhang Chun Xiao, after graduating from Donglu University, returned to Da Yan and obtained a position at the Third Middle School teaching Chinese language. We remained friends.

1 9 3 3

My third daughter was born in February; I named her Rong Xing.

1 9 3 5

Twin boys were born in February; both were healthy. I named them Zhu Xi and Shou Tian. I was so delighted to have twin boys! I held a banquet for the "one-month-old" ceremony with ten tables (with eight guests per table, as was the custom). Relatives, friends, and members of the *Dongjing* Society were invited.

Because I had twin boys, my relatives and friends recommended that I find a suitable godfather for the younger boy. The Clan Mu suggested Guang Xian; Guang Xian was a Naxi and the head monk of a temple situated on Ji Zu, a holy Buddhist mountain in Binchuan County, near Dali.

During the March gathering of the Fur and Leather Society, I was selected as their leader because of my knowledge, experience, and integrity. I served in this capacity for two years. It was a distinct honor to retain the position for a second year; the members trusted me.

During April, because the twins became too much for Yu Ji to breastfeed, I hurriedly looked for a wet nurse. In Jin Shan, a Bai woman, with a young son of her own, was found. She agreed to breast feed Zhu Xi and was given some money. She, and her son, lived in my courtyard for just over one year.

At the June *Dongjing* gathering, I performed the Rite of Lighting a Candle and Making a Wish. I thanked General Guan for sending me the twin boys and wished that General Guan would bless my sons with good health and good luck in the future.

1 9 3 6

During February, the Clan Mu sponsored an outing to Ji Zu. They were so pleased with a wax disk recording of *Dongjing* music made the previous year by Dao Yun Kui, a professor from a German university, that they provided rice and firewood for seventy people for a five-day outing. During the outing, I brought gifts of butter and Tibetan *joss* sticks for my meeting with Guang Xian. Guang Xian agreed to be Shan Tian's godfather.

While we were there, a local Guomindang official told us that we should not remain in that area because the Red Army had entered Yunnan. Immediately, we returned to Da Yan.

In April, Shou Tian, my second twin boy, died of measles. I was shocked and saddened. Guang Xian, his godfather, never saw him. With several boards, I made a coffin and buried him on a wild hill. Mama, Yu Ji, and relatives comforted me as I still had an heir, Zhu Xi, the first twin boy.

One month later, the Red Army approached Da Yan. Wherever the soldiers traveled, they "canvassed" local, wealthy, landlords and merchants for financial contributions. The Qi Wen villagers knew that the year before I had contributed more than the others to the construction of a stone road. That year, I had been the largest contributor to building the Qi Wen school house; my name was the first on the list of benefactors carved on a stone tablet by the grateful villagers. Because of my prominent support for these projects, local communist sympathizers and poor farmers suggested me as one of the landlords to "canvas" for money.

Since I had a good reputation in Qi Wen, the day before the soldiers entered Da Yan some villagers informed me. I had no idea about the Red Army. I learned that other landlords and merchants were hiding to avoid being discovered. I immediately left for Jin Shan and hid in a friend's house. The soldiers remained in Da Yan for five days. They went to Qi Wen searching for me.

While in the Da Yan area, some soldiers gave money to poor farmers. When they left, the Red Army took some people with them as porters. One of my friends, who was head of the post office, did not hide and was taken as a porter. Some weeks later, I was shocked to learn that by the roadside at Shigu my friend was executed. I thought how lucky I was that I was warned and hid. The concerned villagers had, perhaps, saved my life.

Even though the local Guomindang government told the townspeople that the Red Army were robbers and bandits, I did not care. I did not make any judgment about them in my mind.

After a six-month illness of leucorrhea, Mama died on June 2nd, at the age of fifty-six. A Chinese herbal doctor diagnosed the disease but had no efficient medicine. Several Chinese herbal doctors were the only medical service available.

On the day of her demise, I informed close relatives[25] by sending them a long, white cloth gown. The memorial ceremony lasted almost a month. Since my mother had become a Buddhist four years earlier, on the first and second days, I invited eight Buddhist monks to recite *A Mi Tou Jing,* the *Sutra of the Infinite,* in the family chapel to release her soul to heaven. On the second day, the *Dongjing* Society held a ceremony in the evening playing *Ten Offerings* and chanting the *Twenty-four Piety Sutras.* From the third to the twenty-eighth days, our family received guests

The grave of He Yi An's parents.

paying condolence calls. Since my mother came from a wealthy family, her father had been a general, the front and back boards of her coffin were painted red. On the final day, the coffin was carried out of the house and buried in the family graveyard.

My mother's death saddened me greatly and I wanted to cry; but being a real man I swallowed my tears.

I buried my parents together in one tomb. After my mother's death, my only hope was to be a dutiful son by cultivating my moral character, perfecting my temper and myself, and being a real Daoist. I had loved my mother and her passing was a great loss for me.

Before her demise, she asked me to recite the Buddhist *sutras* for her. I learned the *Prajnaparamita Sutra* [26] and included portions of them in my morning *sutra* recitation. Each year on the anniversary of my mother's demise, I ate vegetarian meals and made an offering to her memory.

I now stopped the family fur and leather business. This decision was based upon my sadness at my mother's passing, my worsening relationship with Yu Ji, and, ultimately, my lack of sufficient capital to purchase the raw leather in the winter for the year's work. The masters and apprentices left my courtyard. The family income fell to two hundred silver dollars, plus the land rent income of one hundred silver dollars. Rice still cost seven to eight copper coins per *jin*.

When my parents were alive, I depended upon them for everything. I realized that I had insufficient capital to start my own proper business and, also, that I really was incapable of running my own business. I could have worked as an accountant for wealthy families; however, because I was a well known person locally with a respected social standing, I considered that it would not be socially correct for me to work for others.

With my limited financial resources, my only option was to start a small foodstuffs business. When new rice, new wheat, and other commodities were first available in the market, I bought large quantities of them at low prices and stored them in my courtyard. Later, when the supply of these products diminished and the price rose, I privately informed peddlers what commodities I had for sale. They visited my courtyard to make bulk purchases and subsequently sold them in the market. Using this scheme, I did not have to work as a street peddler and maintained my social respectability.

1 9 3 7

Because *Dongjing* Societies were very popular, members of the ten wealthy, educated families from Jin Shan requested the Da Yan *Dongjing* Society to recommend a teacher for their young sons. On the recommendation of the older Da Yan members and knowing someone in Jin Shan, I was invited. I taught them the music and the Wen Chang *sutras* over a ten-year period. On the sixth day of Spring Festival, some villagers came to my house with an offering of rice, sugar cane, and tea; they bowed before me. Later that day, they carried my bedding to Jin Shan. I lived in the village for one month; during the day the young men worked and I taught them in the evenings. I spent another month after the Torch Festival in June, or July. After several years, I went a third time during the month of December.

At this time, I discovered that Zhu Xi, just over two years old, murmured and did not speak clearly. My neighbors told me a rumor that the family of my son's wet nurse had a disease. They implied that this Bai woman might be the cause of Zhu Xi's health problems.

In March, the Lijiang government organized a day of religious ceremonies to support the Chinese people in their struggle in the Anti-Japanese war.[27] At a ceremony in the Black Dragon Park, the *Dongjing* Society lit *joss* sticks, played music and recited *Deng ke*. The wish was that the gods would help the Chinese people to defeat the Japanese.

An old *lama* held a ceremony reciting incantations in front of straw figure. "Emperor of Japan" was written on a piece of white paper and hung around the figure's neck. After shooting arrows at the figure, he then burnt it. Buddhist monks lit *joss* sticks and held a ceremony in which they wrote their wishes of strength and bravery for the Chinese people in their struggle.

1 9 3 9

After Zhu Xi was four years old, he often lay on the ground and lost control. I realized that my only son had epilepsy and infantile paralysis. I invited Chinese herbal doctors to examine my son and prescribe remedies. None of the remedies worked.

During April, seven masters, who were having problems with their bosses, rented two of the four buildings of my courtyard to start their own shoe business. They established the Solidarity Factory. The monthly rent was eight silver dollars. I continued my foodstuffs business.

That autumn, because of bad weather locally, there was a poor harvest. The food shortage was so severe that some farmers in the villages died of starvation. Some wealthy people of Da Yan, members of the *Dongjing* Society, had the idea to use public money to purchase grains and distribute them to the needy. With the permission of the local government, grains were purchased from neighboring counties and distributed.

1 9 4 0

Rong Xing started the three-year primary school during March. She studied Chinese language, mathematics, calligraphy, singing, art, and physical education. There was no tuition fee but the students purchased their own textbooks. During her three years in higher primary school, she studied Chinese language, mathematics, history, geography, art, physical education, and biology. At the end of each week, there was a gathering for the whole school at which the headmaster stated conclusions about the studies from the past week.

Because of my education and business experience, in April, the members of the Solidarity Factory invited me to join them. I stopped my foodstuffs business and became a partner by investing two hundred silver dollars. The family income fell to forty silver dollars plus the land rent income of one hundred silver dollars and the house rent of ninety-six dollars.

I was able to fulfill my responsibilities as accountant and purchaser of raw materials and still have the time to pursue my active social program. Each year, after Spring Festival, the partners received interest from our investments in the Solidarity Factory. Most of the profit was kept to increase our working capital and each of us received forty silver dollars. A one time land tax of the quantity of grain carried by five horses was levied to support the war effort.

My fourth daughter was born in October.

During December, while teaching in Jin Shan, one evening I was wakened by what seemed to be somebody shouting outside. When I got up and went outside there was silence; nobody was there. When I returned to my room, I heard a sound again as if there was a large fire in Da Yan. I called the young people and we went up to the roof and looked; we saw nothing. So, I knew that the sounds were made by ghosts. I went out and stood in the yard and spoke loudly.

"Good evening everybody. Please do not make trouble. Sometime later when the young men in Jin Shan master the music, I shall set up a *sutra* reciting room to release your souls from purgatory." After I said this, it gradually became quiet.

The Solidarity Factory in He Yi An's courtyard.
From *Forgotten Kingdom* by Peter Goullart, used by permission

Peter Goullart was a central Guomindang government official; he was appointed the Lijiang Depot Manager of the Chinese Industrial Cooperatives. Peter found the Lijiang region conducive for commerce and industry because neither licenses nor permits were required and there were no excise taxes. Two Cooperative regulations had to be met to qualify for technical assistance and a low-interest loan: first, a minimum of seven people to form a cooperative; second, the people must work with their hands.

In June, Peter Goullart heard about the Solidarity Factory and visited my courtyard. After several discussions, Peter learned that our Factory manufactured one style of shoes, using mainly manual labor; our yearly output was two thousand pairs of shoes. Peter agreed to act as a guarantor and we obtained a loan from the local bank to purchase sewing machines, production tools, and raw materials. Peter taught us how to make different styles of shoes, work with different types of leather, and use a shoe mending machine. The Solidarity Factory was given a second name, the Qi Wen Cooperative. Peter trusted me and made me manager.

Peter frequently went on long journeys and asked me to look after his documents and passport. Handicraftsmen often asked me to help them obtain support from Peter. I invited Peter to gatherings of the *Dongjing* Society and for meals at my courtyard; Peter enjoyed listening to the *Dongjing* music, talking, and drinking Naxi red liquor, *Yinjiu*. Peter considered me his best friend in Da Yan.

My fourth daughter died of convulsions in October.

Because of Peter's interest, support, and encouragement, within two years the productivity of the Qi Wen Cooperative increased to a yearly output of four thousand pairs of shoes, of several different styles made with different leathers. This higher production efficiency was achieved by employing machines operated by a trained staff. The shoes sold well in Da Yan because they were of a good quality and priced lower than those manufactured in Shanghai and Kunming. This business success resulted in each partner receiving a yearly income of sixty silver dollars.

In March, hundreds of people started to die from cholera, both Da Yan townspeople and farmers from nearby villages. No precautions were taken by the government officials nor the people. I took no precautions. I was quite active in public affairs at this time and suggested to some friends that we visit the governor of Lijiang with a plan to build coffins. The governor agreed with our plan and sponsored it by providing seven thousand silver dollars of public money. These funds had been donated by a rich Naxi and six coffin makers, members of the *Dongjing* Society. These members organized thirty carpenters to help them make coffins. Simple coffins were provided free for the poor and higher quality coffins were sold to the wealthy at a substantial profit. The profit from these sales was used to buy salt; members of the *Dongjing* Society volunteered to sell the salt; the profits were used for sponsoring our gatherings.

During the cholera epidemic, I came early one morning and discovered that the man who watched over the coffins during the night was frightened. I asked him why he was so frightened. The night watchman replied that he could not sleep during the past night because of the noise coming from one coffin as if some people were preparing to carry it away. He pointed to the coffin, the second in a stack of five. At eight o'clock that morning, a family came to select a coffin. After considering all of the available coffins, they selected the second one in the stack of five!

When the cholera epidemic was almost over, government officials invited local religious leaders to pray to the gods to bless the people. Figures of the five cholera ghosts were constructed from white paper: one with a tiger's skin, one with a head like a cock, one with a body like a man, one with a head like a raven, and one with a head like a donkey. A Daoist priest, wearing straw shoes, lit *joss* sticks, made an offering, and recited *sutras* in front of the white paper figures. He asked the five ghosts to excuse the people. After this ceremony, the five paper ghosts were burnt. Monks, lamas, and *dongba* then held their ceremonies.

My fifth daughter was born in May; I named her Quan Xing.

During the summer, a local government official came to my courtyard and spoke to the members of the Qi Wen Cooperative. "Your country has trouble. Your incomes are good. Please contribute." he requested. We donated two hundred silver dollars towards the anti-Japanese war effort; this was a voluntary contribution and there were no extra taxes.

1 9 4 4

During this year, the first son of the Clan Mu and I were both thirty-six years old. During the Sanduo Festival (See Appendix p. 137), February 8th, I asked my friend to take a salted pig's head and a cock to the Sanduo Temple and make an offering for me that god may bless me and protect me during this unlucky year. The Clan Mu invited me and my friends to participate in a seven day banquet so I held no birthday banquet.

1 9 4 6

I had been content with my marriage of twenty years; there were three surviving children from eight births. Despite the consultation of many Chinese herbal doctors about Zhu Xi's health, there was no change. My weak son had epilepsy and no hope to be healthy; this left me without an heir. Because Yu Ji was too old to give me another son, she agreed that I take a second wife. I also obtained permission from Yu Ji's family, her brother. I told my two daughters, Rong Xing and Quan Xing, that a new mother would come because I wanted a healthy son, an heir. Most men did not ask permission but took a second wife secretly. A relative suggested that I marry Yang Shang Yuan, a widow, twelve years younger than me. Shang Yuan's mother-in-law

Shang Yuan and He Yi An.

demanded twenty grams of gold for her; an unreasonable amount, but I paid.

Shang Yuan lived with her mother, not with her mother-in-law. Because I was concerned that somebody from the mother-in-law's family might ask for more money, I arranged for Shang Yuan to join me without the mother-in-law knowing. On June 13, I informed Shang Yuan to be ready the next evening after supper. The next day, I acted as usual. After a discussion with my partners at the Qi Wen Cooperative, I had my lunch. During the afternoon, I visited a friend. I had my usual supper with my six partners and then they went to meet Shang Yuan. She wore clean clothes and stood in front of her mother's house where my partners met her. They escorted her back to my courtyard. My family placed a table with fruits, sweets, and candies to receive her. For such an "escape marriage," there was no ceremony, no certificate, only an agreement between the man and the woman. Some days later, she returned to her mother's to collect her things.

After the marriage, I lived in the middle room, with Yu Ji in the room to the right, Shang Yuan in the room to the left; I slept with both women for one year. For a short time, Yu Ji and Shang Yuan had a good relationship and worked together weaving clothes. I asked Yu Ji to return some of the jewelry sent to her by my parents as gifts before our marriage. I sold the jewelry for capital to do business as my money was invested in the Qi Wen Cooperative. I then asked Yu Ji for some of her money to use as capital to do business. Yu Ji objected. We quarreled because of the money. From then on, I lived alone with Shang Yuan.

Generally, I provided no support for Yu Ji and her two daughters. Sometimes, I gave them some of the land rent money. I did not make much money because I usually went to the *Dongjing*

Society and seldom spent time working. I could only afford to support one wife.

Yu Ji and Rong Xing grew vegetables and sold them in the market. To support themselves, they worked as peddlers in the street selling tea, sugar, and soap; their monthly income was just sufficient for them to live. Spring Festival 1946 was the last large family celebration. After this, Yu Ji, Rong Xing, and Quan Xing did not enter the family chapel.

I had come to a turning point in my life. I was becoming older and did not have the strength as when I was younger and active in public affairs. When I was young, I lived off my parents. When they died, they had left me some money; I had spent all this money. Thus, the bad state of the family economy and my worsening relationship with Yu Ji troubled me. Because the *Dongjing sutras* were a major part of my life, I directed my energy and attention away from public affairs, away from my family and into the activities of the *Dongjing* Society. I was the leader of a group of ten members who kept the *Dongjing* Society functioning. Despite all the tension produced by my family and financial troubles, through my concentration on the *sutras* my mind became calm and peaceful.

Faced with difficulty, one must live on; no use to always cry.

The social trend was quite bad at this time. Men smoked poppy, gambled secretly, and went to prostitutes. Members of the *Dongjing* Society must maintain a good moral virtue; if not, other members would look down on them.

Dr. Heinz Breitkreuz, a German medical doctor, traveling in Yunnan, stayed in Da Yan for two months. Peter Goullart arranged for him to examine my son, Zhu Xi. After examining

the boy, he wrote a prescription, which I took to "Missionary
Mu," a British missionary. He gave me three bottles of white
tablets. Zhu Xi took the tablets and had no seizures or fits.
Hearing of the success of his treatment, "Missionary Mu" told
me that he would write to a friend in Shanghai asking him to
send a supply of tablets. I thanked him with gifts of eggs and
hens. Two months later when all the tablets were finished, the
seizures and fits returned. No tablets ever arrived from
Shanghai. The boy's condition became worse.

There were no communists in Da Yan. We only knew the
Guomindang government. The people obeyed the government.
During the years of Chinese Civil War (1945-49)[28], common people only took care of themselves; people did not look for trouble.
The Guomindang government needed new soldiers and recruited young men from Da Yan; they came four times a year. The
selection depended upon the village head; many families protest-
ed and gave money instead. If there was only one son in the family, he would not be taken. If a son was recruited and ran away,
his father was imprisoned; if a neighbor was imprisoned, nobody
cared. Life in the countryside was much worse than in Da Yan.
Farmers were tenants paying rent; they had no rent income.
During these years, I did not read the newspaper nor follow the
events of the civil war. I was not interested. The *Dongjing* Society
and my music were my life. Nothing else mattered.

1 9 4 7

I now considered that the young men in Jin Shan had mastered the *Dongjing* music because they could proceed through
the entire gathering protocol. So the Da Yan *Dongjing* Society
sent them *sutras* and instruments. The villagers built a tent and

invited the Da Yan *Dongjing* Society. After our celebration of Wen Chang's birthday in Da Yan, we traveled to Jin Shan on February 8th to hold another three-day gathering to celebrate Wen Chang's birthday. After the gathering, I said to the air, "Everyone please have a good time in the Heaven. Afterwards, no matter where or when we play the *Dongjing* music we hope that you all will be well in the Heaven."

At my request, one of the young men had boiled Chinese herbs and porridge; he poured the mixture on the road to kill the ghosts' sickness and hunger. After that the village was never haunted again.

Quan Xing started to attend kindergarten in March.

Later in March, I went to Kunming for business and sight-seeing. During the visit, a wealthy Naxi friend from Da Yan, a Kunming bank manager, arranged an invitation from the provincial broadcasting station to record a flute solo of *Spring has Come*, *Waves Washing the Sand,* and *Song of a Water Dragon*. Later, I went to the Hundred Generations Company to record five pieces of flute solo on a wax disc. While walking in the street, I heard my recording broadcast on the radio. Naxi friends living in Kunming admired me and were proud of me.

My first son with Shang Yuan was born on June 10th.

In November, my friend Zhang Chun Xiao died of lung disease.

1 9 4 8

During the past two years, the relationship between Yu Ji and Shang Yuan, my two wives, had deteriorated. They quarreled about who should get Mama's clothes and numerous other petty things. Because of this bad relationship, during February, Shang Yuan and I moved into the two rooms of my courtyard which faced the street. We opened a shop and started a small business selling grain, salt, cayenne, tea, liquor, and other dried foods. Since Shang Yuan could run the shop by herself, I continued as manager of the Qi Wen Cooperative. After moving to the shop, I seldom gave any money to support Yu Ji and her two daughters. To support themselves, they continued to work as street peddlers.

Because there was no chapel in the shop, I changed the time of my *sutra* recitation. I went to sleep at eight o'clock and woke at midnight. I sat up in my bed, crossed my legs, closed my eyes, breathed calmly, and recited quietly to myself for thirty minutes the *sutra* book *Opening Prayer*. In my mind, I thought about the *sutra*, pronounced it correctly, and stood respectfully beside Wen Chang. Afterwards, for Mama, I recited portions from the *prajnaparamita sutra*.

My first daughter with Shang Yuan was born in July. I named her Lian Di, which means "Son to follow."

1 9 4 9

In April, the Lijiang Guomindang government started to lose administrative control to the communist guerrilla forces. Da Yan was in confusion. Nobody knew what was going to happen. The townspeople were not aware that there was a new China. A communist China. However, the local farmers knew all about the new China from the communist guerrillas. The plans to distribute the land and wealth rallied the farmers to active participation in the "liberation" movement.

The first time the Red Army came to Da Yan in 1936, the Guomindang government told the people that the soldiers were bandits who wanted to punish the wealthy. Many landlords and merchants, including myself, had hidden and escaped without any harm.

The second time, when the People's Liberation Army entered Da Yan July 1st, the Lijiang Communist Party organized a large celebration meeting to welcome them. Thousands of people attended. There were so many people and so much noise that I could not hear the speeches. I returned home realizing that the old Guomindang government had been defeated and that a new society would appear. What type of new society I had no idea. As Lijiang had been "liberated" peacefully, I was not afraid.

Most of the new local government leaders were not from Da Yan. They acted immediately by imprisoning, or executing, some wealthy people and those of social position. In Da Yan and the surrounding villages, cadres from the new government told the people that they should support the new government. More importantly, all old ceremonies and gatherings were forbidden! The new government believed that they all were based upon feudal superstition. I was so frightened by this warning that I did not dare celebrate, on July 10th, the Festival of Accepting and Sending Back Ancestral Spirits.

A new government ruling stated that all things must be sold in shops, nothing could be sold on the street. Therefore, Yu Ji and Rong Xing could not work as peddlers. To support themselves, they worked at odd jobs, mainly physical labor. They earned twenty-five copper coins each day. Rice cost eight copper coins per *jin*.

A member of the *Dongjing* Society who had been involved in revolutionary activities became a government official. Secretly, he warned the members of the *Dongjing* Society not to hold their August 3rd gathering. "The new government controls everything!" he told us. "They believe that the activities of the *Dongjing* Society have something to do with feudal superstition. They are forbidden. You must obey them."

With this stern warning, the planned gathering and all subsequent *Dongjing* Society activities were canceled. I stopped doing *qigong* as my mind was neither calm nor quiet. No Confucian gathering was held in September.

At the end of 1949 and the beginning of 1950 the government introduced a policy for reducing rents and returning deposits plus interest. The rents were to be reduced by twenty-five percent and the deposits and interest since 1937 returned. As a result of this policy, many wealthy people became poor. Many of them and many local "fancy people" were jailed. Many were members of the *Dongjing* Society. Some went mad. Others committed suicide.

As a part of this government policy, the new Lijiang County governor was combing out bandits and opposing local despots. This was aimed at anti-revolutionary elements. Prominent, wealthy landlords were jailed. Some were executed. The government pursued a policy of "kill a chicken to frighten a monkey;" a chicken is easy to catch and kill, a monkey is loud, stubborn, and does not listen.

Even with these warnings, I still did not comprehend the significance of the new China. I considered all officials, all governments, to be the same. I thought that living as I did before, paying my taxes, obeying the laws, the new government should not cause me any trouble.

1 9 5 0

In January, my first son with Shang Yuan suddenly died of convulsions. I was shocked. I was very fond of the boy. There was no ceremony and the body was buried on a wild hill. Again, I faced the predicament of not having an heir.

I believed that most landlords were good people; we saved the farmers' lives. I had never done any harm to others. If there was a bad harvest, I reduced, or canceled, my rents. The idea that the farmers were exploited by the landlords was planted in their heads by the Communist cadres. In Qi Wen, there were eight wealthy families out of thirty-seven. Members of three of these wealthy, landlord families had treated their tenant farmers badly, one from a fourth wealthy family had opened a poppy house. With the local farmers' instigation, these four were executed. These executions frightened me. However, I remained calm. I told myself that I had done many good things, contributed money for repairing bridges and mending roads, building schools. The new government officials must know this and, perhaps, would not cause me trouble. I lost my position as manager of the Qi Wen Cooperative and the new government appointed a young person as accountant.

For Spring Festival, the new government said that the people should not spend a lot of time nor consume a lot of food. Young men volunteered to go around to each family to check if they were boiling meat. They visited my courtyard to check on my activities. I was afraid to perform any of the extensive annual family ceremonies throughout Spring Festival. No trip was made to the family graveyard on the third day. The shops were not closed for the customary fifteen day holiday.

I believed that it was the thought that was important. A major celebration, or gathering, was not necessary. If I had no banquet, but just drank a cup of tea, ate a simple meal, and in my mind asked Wen Chang to bless me, I believed that Wen Chang would be satisfied with me.

Quan Xing started primary school in March. There were forty boys and girls in her class.

In March, the new government organized some musicians to form a Music Society which was divided into four groups; each group had seven or eight members. The first group were members of the *Dongjing* Society with myself as their leader. The second group were members of the Huangjing Society. The third group were citizens and the fourth group young students. Most members of the first three groups could play instruments. But the young students knew only new songs praising the new government.

Each week, there were two activities: on Wednesday, group one was in charge of finding a place and arranging the program; they played music or were taught new songs by the students. On Saturday, group two was responsible for the arrangements. We played at Spring Festival, Lijiang Martyrs' Day, the anniversary of the founding of new China (October 1st), at meetings of government officials, and when a high official of the central government died.

During the Korean War, in August, the Music Society performed for five days at the Luo Ma Hui, the Cattle Fair, to encourage people to contribute money to support the army. Those who contributed could write their names on a large piece of white cloth; the cloth was later displayed as a banner. While playing, I overheard some farmers talking about now that liberation had come all the wealthy people would be punished. "Those land-lords, we shall cut them into pieces!" said one farmer.

I became very frightened. Very nervous. This was the first time after liberation that I realized that bad things were coming for me. I was not prepared for this.

Life became hard but I could manage it. At the end of 1950, the political movement of reducing rents and returning deposits was pursued actively in Da Yan. Very wealthy landlords, with large land holdings, were the initial target. Twenty wealthier members of the *Dongjing* Society were imprisoned.

I continued to recite my *sutras* at midnight for about thirty minutes. I worked at odd jobs over the next four years carrying bricks and digging sand. I earned ¥0.40 per day.[29] Shang Yuan sold liquor and salt in the small shop and earned ¥1.00 per day. She sold the items on consignment from private businessmen so that no capital was necessary. Our ¥40 per month was spent purchasing food for Shang Yuan, Lian Di, and myself.

The Music Society.

Vegetables, mainly potatoes, were available only from the government vegetable cooperative. A person's daily quota was decided by the salesperson. They actively discriminated against landlord families. Some days, I could see vegetables in the shop, had money to pay for them, but the salesperson would not sell them to me. When I worked in the countryside, on my way home I purchased vegetables from farmers.

1 9 5 1

In July, the Farmers' Association[30] of Dong Yuan, where I owned land, sent three armed farmers to find me and bring me to the village. I took rice with me and ate and slept in a large room with about thirty other landowners. The Farmers' Association asked us privately to confess orally the bad things that we had done to the local farmers. We were controlled by armed farmers. Each day, the Farmers' Association organized political study for us. We were asked to state our attitudes; before liberation, we had taken money from the poor farmers which was wrong; now, we wanted to return the money. Sometimes, we were read policies and documents from the central government.

The Lijiang County Committee told us that if we admitted our bad deeds, we would be punished slightly. If we refused, we would be punished severely. "If you correct your mistakes, you can provide the opportunity to reform yourself and become a new person" we were informed. I admitted all my bad deeds and was not punished.

In the middle of August, the Dong Yuan Farmers' Association sent an official with me to visit my courtyard in Qi Wen and make an inventory of all my possessions. The upstairs rooms were then locked. Nothing was confiscated at this time. The Farmers' Association kept investigating those landlords who they still suspected and had not admitted their bad deeds. Some landlords, friends of mine, were beaten. Some were jailed. Others were executed. When the Farmers' Association considered that a landlord had a good attitude, meaning he agreed to return the land, and to repay the rents by selling his possessions, then the Farmers' Association allowed him to return home.

During August while I was locked up, Yu Ji was notified that Shang Yuan had been locked up in Hong Wei. The Hong Wei Farmers' Association claimed that the Fur and Leather Society had taken excessive rents from the farmers for the forty *mu* of land they had owned in Hong Wei. I had been leader of the Society during 1935-1937 and, therefore, I was one of those responsible. As I was already locked up in Dong Yuan, the Farmers' Association took Shang Yuan in my place. When Rong Xing brought me my food, she informed me about Shang Yuan's lock up. During the two months Shang Yuan was locked up, Rong Xing and Quan Xing took her food.

As things were not strict at this time, I asked to be released for a day to resolve the situation in Hong Wei. After receiving permission, I went to my house in Qi Wen and collected some earrings and rings that I had hidden and went to Hong Wei to negotiate with the Farmers' Association. After completing my negotiations in Hong Wei, I returned to my lock up in Dong Yuan. At the end of September, Shang Yuan was released.

Since I had demonstrated a good attitude and agreed to reduce my tenants' rents by twenty-five percent and return their deposits, I was released in October and returned to Qi Wen. The Dong Yuan Farmers' Association reminded me three times about the money that I had promised. I withdrew my ¥200 from the Qi Wen Cooperative and gave it to them. This was not enough. To satisfy their financial demands, Shang Yuan and I had to sell my quota of shoes and all the furniture and copper ware from the downstairs rooms of my courtyard.

The land reform movement started in the autumn of 1951. The Farmers' Association asked the poor farmers' advice to classify people. The Farmers' Association staff wrote their suggestions for each person on a piece of paper. After going through this procedure three times, the Farmers' Association classified people into landlords, middle class peasants, and poor farmers. The Qi Wen Farmers' Association advised Shang Yuan, since she was young, to divorce me and be classified as a normal farmer and not as a landlord. She did not take their advice, remained my wife, and was classified as a landlord.

During the land reform movement, Yu Ji was also classified as a landlord. Because the Farmers' Association considered her an honest person and knew how I treated her, they did not deal harshly with her. As I myself was working at odd jobs, I had no money to give Yu Ji and her two daughters. To support themselves, they continued to work at odd jobs.

During my lock up in Dong Yuan, my stepmother was frightened for my safety and became ill; she died in December. Up to this time, she had lived by herself in a room in my family courtyard. She supported herself with some private money. Sometimes I sent her food from the small shop. After liberation, the economy in Da Yan was very poor. Generally, according to Naxi tradition, the coffin should be placed at home for some days for the family to receive their friends, relatives, and neighbors. No funeral ceremony was held because there was not enough money and the new government did not allow such ceremonies. I was afraid to be criticized.

I informed the Farmers' Association of her demise. The day after her demise, two armed farmers watched the corpse being placed into the coffin; they checked that no treasures were placed in the coffin. On the third day, I just hired eight sedan men to carry the coffin, and buried it in the family graveyard simply and quietly. The two armed farmers escorted the porters to the graveyard and watched to make sure the coffin was not tampered with before being buried. After the burial, the two armed farmers returned to Qi Wen.

1 9 5 3

The food distribution system was started by the government. Each person was assigned a food quota from the bureau and issued a food certificate. The food certificate was valid at government grain shops in the locality where the person resided. Before liberation, the rich ate meat and rice; the poor ate corn pies. Annually, the poor townspeople and farmers could only afford to purchase a small amount of rice, usually at Spring Festival. This new system gave everyone equal access to rice, wheat, and corn. Each adult received a monthly quota of thirty *jin* (fifteen kilograms); ten *jin* of rice, ten *jin* of wheat, and ten *jin* of corn. These grains were sold at government subsidized prices. In addition, each person received a household identification book which was valid only for a specific residence.

My second lock up was with twenty other landlords in Qi Wen in November. Shang Yuan was able to send me food.

The Farmers' Association started to focus on urban administration, so it was renamed the Street Committee. The Street Committee said that I had exploited the farmers' properties before liberation. The Street Committee treated the wealthy landlords very badly to discover the locations of their hidden treasures. Many were tortured; I was not.

Each evening there was a meeting. Most evenings there was political study. Some evenings, members of the Street Committee met with the local farmers to discuss the landlords in the next room. One evening, I overheard them. One member asked the farmers about a landlord's previous conduct.

"Was he really a bad landlord?" "Yes! Yes!", they replied. "Should we punish him?" "Yes! Yes!" "Should we execute him?" "Yes! Yes!"

Some landlords were executed. I was extremely frightened that one day I could be executed because this group of farmers agreed that I was a bad landlord.

The Qi Wen Street Committee told me that I must repay the local farmers' deposits. With a good attitude, cooperation, and payment of the market value of two thousand *jin* of rice, I would be treated well. Otherwise, bad trouble. Two years earlier, I had reduced rents and sold all my possessions to return deposits for the Dong Yuan farmers. Beside my courtyard property, I had nothing left.

During my second lock up, in December, Shang Yuan informed me that Zhu Xi, my sickly son, had died. There was no funeral ceremony because there was not enough money and the new government forbade such activities. I was afraid to be criticized. Since I had no money for a coffin, I suggested to Shang Yuan that she use some floor boards to make a coffin. This was not allowed. I then suggested that she use my long, white cotton gown to cover the body and bury him secretly. Shang Yuan, Yu Ji, Rong Xing, and Quan Xing buried the body.

At that moment, I felt that almost everything was over. I had lost my heir, my agricultural properties, most of my possessions. I had no reason to live.

Death was nothing to me. I was spiritually prepared for death and told Shang Yuan, "If I die, find a way for yourself."

Later, I decided that I must find the courage to manage to live for Shang Yuan who treated me so well, and my young daughter, Lian Di. At midnight, I often recited to myself the *Incantation of Body Purification* asking Wen Chang to bless me, to protect me, and to give me the strength to overcome my present difficulties.

I feel terribly upset
There are thirty-six thousand deities fighting in my mind
No matter when a new doom falls
I shall behave as usual
I shall always keep Wen Chang in my mind
I shall purify myself often
When I encounter catastrophes again
I wish I could survive forever
Wen Chang bless me

Realizing my desperate situation, I asked to meet with the leader of the Street Committee. At that meeting, I made the following offer, "I suggest that you start with my house; after, I shall live by my own hands." I suggested that they sell my property to repay the farmers' deposits. I volunteered to be an example for the others and, perhaps, achieve a good result. The chairman informed the County Governor's Committee that I had a good attitude towards the land reform. In late December, a member of the Qi Wen Street Committee went to my courtyard and posted a notice on the front gate stating that this property had been confiscated and was now public property. Many properties were confiscated at this time.

Several days later, I was taken to my courtyard where the Street Committee had called a meeting of the local farmers. My whole family knelt down in the center of the courtyard with the farmers around us. An official addressed the gathering.

"This family were landlords in the past. They took many things away from you. Today, we shall take back these many things." The official then turned to me.

"Please forgive me! Please forgive me!" I replied.

The upstairs rooms were then unlocked and all the furniture and the decorations moved into the courtyard. They were distributed to the farmers as the "fruits of victory." I was distraught to see a farmer take the copper statues of Xuan Tian, Guan Yin, and Wen Chang. The statues had been purchased sixty years earlier by my grandfather and worshiped by him, my father, and myself.

1 9 5 4

In January, I was in the first group of landlords to be released and allowed to return home. After my second lock up, I did not participate in the Music Society; the Music Society stopped its activities because most members of the first two groups were locked up. Music was provided by professional musicians at the celebrations.

My second daughter with Shang Yuan was born in March; I named her Qian Di.

The People's Liberation Army advertised for new recruits. Rong Xing wanted to join. She was told that she would not be considered because her father was a landlord.

In April, the Street Committee took possession of my courtyard. The leader of the Street Committee told me, "Because you admitted your bad deeds, you have a good attitude, we shall give you a house to live in. If you had not admitted your bad deeds, you would live in a cave."

My family and I, including Yu Ji and her two daughters, were assigned to live in a stable. When I was first shown the stable, pigs were kept in the two lower rooms and the two upper rooms were completely open. After the pigs were removed, Shang Yuan and I cleaned the two lower rooms thoroughly. To enclose the two upper rooms, we borrowed a wooden form for making bricks, carried soil from the river, made soil bricks and constructed walls.

On the day we left the courtyard, all family members were searched by armed farmers to ensure that we did not conceal any money or jewelry. The members of the Qi Wen Co-operative were ordered to move out of the courtyard to a new location. Shang Yuan, Lian Di, Qian Di, and I lived downstairs while Yu Ji, Rong Xing, and Quan Xing lived upstairs.

Life became miserable when we moved to the stable.[31] Shang Yuan and I had only the clothes that we were wearing and several pots and bowls. No furniture. We had to cope with these conditions with our two-month-old daughter, Qian Di. We could afford only a little flour and bean curd residue for our meals; sometimes edible plants were included in our meager diet. We were always hungry. I accepted living in the stable as my reality; I was under control and could do nothing.

In early 1954, landlords were required to perform "volunteer labor." This involved cleaning the streets and rivers two to three times a month. In the early years after liberation, many beggars without families often died on the street; the volunteer labor included the removal and burial of these bodies as well as dead animals. Shang Yuan and I were enlisted and participated in this landlord labor force after our move to the stable.

During the next three years, Shang Yuan and I worked mainly at odd jobs. We shouldered pears and sold them in the market. When the pear season finished, we cut wood in the mountains and sold it in the market. Eventually, to support ourselves, we performed manual labor, digging sand.

I realized how drastically my life had changed in just five years. Before liberation, I received both business and rent incomes. My days were filled with *Dongjing* Society gatherings and activities, frequent social invitations, and many family festivals. Just five years after liberation, my days were filled with exhausting physical labor. I was no longer a man of means.

A man of leisure, a man of pleasure, had, out of necessity, become a man of the street. I lived from hand to mouth. Being seen doing physical labor on the street was a profound embarrassment for me. Participating in the volunteer labor was humiliating. These were the worst years of my life.

1 9 5 5

Just before Spring Festival, Shang Yuan and I worked at odd jobs; there was a lot of construction and odd jobs were easy to find. Yu Ji was mending brushes; Rong Xing and Quan Xing worked at odd jobs. Food prices were almost the same as before liberation. Rice cost ¥0.07 per *jin*. However, since I had lost my business and rent incomes I had almost no money to purchase food.

For New Year's Eve, I held no ceremony; I bought a small piece of meat, boiled it and with some vegetables and had a simple meal with Shang Yuan, Lian Di, and Qian Di. Yu Ji, Rong Xing, and Quan Xing celebrated separately. The first day of Spring Festival was also a holiday and the following day we returned to work.

1 9 5 7

My family and I ate in the public dining room[32] of the Qi Wen Street Committee. Those serving the food often discriminated against the landlords giving us and our families less food than our allotment and more to their own relatives and friends. Because of our hunger, each morning Lian Di and Qian Di waited by the river to collect any leftovers thrown in by others, usually small pieces of animal intestine and vegetable leaves. These items were boiled and supplemented our meager diet.

At this time, to support themselves, Yu Ji and her two daughters continued to work at odd jobs. They wore rough clothes and straw shoes. Usually, they woke early and worked all day until late in the evening. Sometimes, they worked all night planting rice seed. They lived a hand to mouth existence; their diet was whatever they could afford but there was never enough food, and they found themselves always hungry.

In April, the Street Committee considered that perhaps they had treated me too severely and hinted several times that I could work in the Fur Cooperative of Da Yan. I sent my application to the Da Yan Committee and the Administration Bureau of Handicrafts. After permission came, I went to work; there were about thirty persons. I was quite familiar with them, some were masters, friends, some neighbors or former apprentices. I worked long hours with little rest; I even worked Sundays while the others had a holiday. I was paid by piece work.

After I joined the Fur Cooperative, I ate in the Cooperative's public dining room. There were two meals a day: a dish and a soup, the amount of rice was limited. After September, people were permitted to eat at home. My family and I purchased food tickets, took our food home and prepared our meals, rice and vegetables, to our taste.

Life became better. Finally enough food. Gone was the constant hungry feeling.

My second son with Shang Yuan was born in June; I named him Yi Xing, meaning that the whole family will have a new beginning. I felt quite happy. Before and after his birth, I recited quietly in my mind the *sutra* book *Opening Prayer*.

In July, Yi Xing became malnourished and developed oedema. I had barely enough money for food for my family. Most of my relatives avoided me on the street for fear of being criticized. At the hospital, a consultation and medicine would cost at least ¥2. So, Yi Xing was fed sugar and pig oil. We asked Shang Yuan's nephew for medicine.

At this time, I was digging soil to enlarge the Black Dragon Park. There was no water in the park. However, one day, by chance, I came across a pool and discovered a toad and a fish. I hid them in my jacket and later took them home. I boiled the toad and fish and fed them to Yi Xing. I prayed to Wen Chang to bless my son. Yi Xing gradually recovered and became healthy.

Lian Di went to primary school for one year. She studied Chinese language, art, physical education, and politics. There was no tuition and the textbooks had been changed after liberation. Each week there was a political conference for teachers and students at which they studied political documents. The government encouraged the teachers and students to make political propaganda. She attended for only one year because she was required to baby-sit Qian Di and Yi Xing.

1 9 5 8

The Anti-Rightist movement[33] established "the four types of people" by adding evildoers and rightists to the landlords and wealthy farmers. Since 1953, during the land reform, I had been labeled as a landlord and lived at the lowest level in society. My classification could not go any lower. I had lost all my possessions. So, this political movement had little effect upon me. During this movement, many landlords were driven to the countryside. Yu Ji was accused of using corn flour to feed pigs. This false accusation resulted in Yu Ji, Rong Xing, and Quan Xing being sent to Puji village where they worked as farmers for three years.

1 9 5 9

Qian Di started to attend primary school. Thirty boys and girls were in her class; four were from former landlord families. The teacher told her class that these four students could not choose their families; however, they could decide their futures. The teacher was honest and did not discriminate against them. Sometimes, the other students scolded them, or even hit them; the four did not report these actions to the teacher. Chinese language, mathematics, physical training, and singing political songs were the four courses.

For breakfast, Shang Yuan prepared *baba*, with corn flour, and tea. In the morning, there were three lessons between eight and eleven o'clock. Qian Di returned home for lunch. Shang Yuan, or Lian Di prepared fried potatoes, salted vegetables, and rice with corn. In the afternoon, there were two lessons from two-thirty until five o'clock. The lunch menu was repeated for supper.

Qian Di enjoyed school very much. I told her that a person with a good education had a bright future. She studied in the evenings and was not allowed to go out. Sometimes, I taught her to read and write Chinese. I told her about my life when I was young, how well my parents had treated me, and how I had contributed money to public projects. Qian Di was the best student in her class.

The government introduced a new policy to deal with the four types of people; they could no longer work at any state-owned, or collective, units. The leader of the Fur and Leather Factory had documents from the upper administration that this new ruling applied to me and I must leave the Factory. In August, a Factory Security Official accompanied me to the Street Committee and asked them to take control of me.

The Street Committee first assigned me to a street renovating team. I worked at odd jobs. Once, I worked at the Quan Pou Power Station with my team for about four months. I felt extremely tired. After the construction was over, the whole team, except me, was assigned to another construction job. I went to the Street Committee to ask for another job. They said that I could do fur and leather work alone. I was told to look for ragged fur and sew it in the courtyard of the Street Committee. They undertook the responsibility to sell my products. Later, the Street Committee said that I could invite others to work with me. I suggested He Da, a former Guomindang official; they agreed.

Several months later, the head of the Street Committee complained that our ragged fur smelled badly and affected their political study. So, we moved out and found a shop in the street. I worked long hours with no holidays; the work was troublesome, sewing small pieces together. However, because I was working freely I felt better. The Street Committee organized a job for Shang Yuan making brushes.

1 9 6 2

In March, Mao Ji Zeng came from Beijing to Da Yan to record *Da Dongjing Xian Jing* music. First Mao invited the Huangjing Society to perform. But their leader did not organize well, they did not have good percussion instruments, and were not well informed about the *Da Dongjing Xian Jing*. So a local calligrapher, Zhang Kui Guang, recommended me and four others from the *Dongjing* Society. We were not invited initially because of our social backgrounds. After obtaining permission from the leader of the prefecture, we took part in the seven day recording session.

I had not held an instrument in my hands nor played *Dongjing* music for twelve years. I played the ten gongs. We chanted the *sutras* and played *Ten Offerings* and *Bagua*.

In April, the Qi Wen Street Committee called a meeting for over eighty people with former landlords, ordinary people, and an official from the Lijiang Public Security Bureau. At the meeting, the leader of the Street Committee said "Now we shall pick two 'persons with caps' (landlords)." He pointed to me and another landlord. "These two no longer have their caps and are ordinary citizens. They can enjoy their rights as ordinary citizens."

Then, the Public Security Bureau official handed each of us a piece of paper stating, "From today, you are considered an ordinary citizen. You share the same rights as other ordinary citizens. You have the rights of election."

We were told that our good attitude during the land reform

He Yi An playing the Ten Gongs.

movement, volunteering to be among the first landlords to give up our houses, and our subsequent good behavior resulted in this reclassification. I was pleased because people would stop treating me as a landlord. While I was classified as a landlord, many people were afraid to talk with me because they might get into trouble. This barrier was removed.

Since the land reform movement, landlords had to attend almost daily political study sessions and were forced, two to three times each month, to participate in volunteer labor. In reality, I was still considered a landlord but did not have to attend the political sessions nor participate in volunteer labor. Shang Yuan was still classified as a landlord; because of this, she had to participate in the volunteer labor until 1978.

1 9 6 3

In April, Qian Xing was married. Yang Qi, her fiancé, had obtained a certificate from his work unit agreeing to the marriage. With this document, they went to the Street Committee to register their marriage and obtain their formal certificate.

Around ten o'clock on their wedding day, Yang Qi and ten of his friends came to the stable. Qian Xing's family accepted the guests at a table with sweets, sunflower and pumpkin seeds, and tea. No firecrackers. No ceremony.

After about one hour, the wedding party, including her brother and sisters, walked to Yang Qi's house. Because both his parents were dead, there was no ceremony. They ate sweets and drank tea. One of Yang Qi's friends made an announcement, "These two people are married and we offer our congratulations." During the afternoon, they drank liquor and talked. Her female friends made the wedding bed, placed flowers in the room, and arranged a display of the gifts. The guests left around five o'clock.

There was no banquet because the government was still combing out the four types of people. People were cautious of political movements. If they held a banquet, the Street Committee might hold a meeting to criticize the family of still living in a bourgeois style.

1 9 6 4

In February, a woman cadre from the Administration Bureau of Handicrafts came to our shop and said that the central government had a policy not allowing private persons to engage in capitalism. She went to negotiate with the Street Committee and the Fur and Leather Factory. So He Da and I entered the Fur and Leather Factory in March. I was assigned the job of softening leather in water and cutting it into thinner pieces. It was a dirty job that required more energy than mending. I continued in this position, at the same salary of ¥19 per month, until 1971.

1 9 6 5

In early 1965, Qian Xing learned that a unit was looking for a cook. She wanted to apply for the position. The leader of the unit would not accept her application. He was afraid that his unit may get into trouble if he employed a girl from a landlord's family.

After this, several families applied to the Street Committee to employ Rong Xing or Qian Xing as baby-sitters. The Street Committee would not consider these applications because they were from a landlord's family. They must do physical labor.

There were many new job opportunities. Often young people with no education, who could not even write their names, obtained these new jobs because their parents were farmers. But temporary odd jobs, usually physical labor, were all that Rong Xing and Qian Xing were allowed to do. They lost all possibilities of a proper, full time, job because I had been a landlord. They had no chance. This was a typical experience for landlords' children.

1 9 6 6

The Cultural Revolution started. Many people went mad. Each day, for three months, they attended political study, marched in the streets, and seldom went to work. Despite not working, people still received their wages.

There was almost nothing in the market, no agricultural produce. However, the grain quotas were maintained. There were long lines for everything in the shops; one required a ticket to purchase anything, be it soap, meat, or clothing. A meat ticket was good only for the month indicated. Each person could buy only one meter of cloth a year.

During this time China became weaker; the people did a lot of harm to the country.

A new phase of the Cultural Revolution started in Da Yan with the middle school students forming revolutionary groups, the Red Guards. All the schools were closed. The student groups quarreled with one another. At political meetings, they criticized the local leaders. The Red Guards believed that some landlords still had money or jewelry hidden in their clothing or buried. To retrieve such treasures, at night the Red Guards suddenly attacked landlords, sometimes physically, to discover their hiding places. Stories of these attacks frightened the four types of people. Everywhere and everything in their homes was searched.

The Red Guards searched Yu Ji's rooms and discovered ¥1000. Yu Ji told them that during the 1950s and 1960s she and her two daughters had worked hard, lived frugally, and managed to save this money. She was criticized and the Street Committee confiscated the money.

Once, I was attacked by the Red Guards. I invited them to search everywhere. I had nothing hidden. I had no fear of physical danger. I treated them politely and had no problem.

At the Fur and Leather Factory during the day there was often political study;[34] I did not attend but did my work. I did not receive Mao's book[35] nor copper medals.

During this time, I was criticized by workers in the Fur and Leather Factory. Had I ever kept Peter Goullart's passport? Did I have a good relationship with Peter? Was my photograph in Peter's book *Forgotten Kingdom?* Because of my relationship with Peter and because of my class element, I was denounced and made the target of a "struggle meeting." The workers forced me to stand for over two hours in the center of the room during a meeting.

"Admit all the evil things from before," one worker said. Another worker spoke evil about me. I admitted to all the false accusations, regretted having done such evil, and asked to be forgiven. Failure to admit "evil deeds" resulted in physical beatings. I was never beaten. These activities, although humiliating, did not frighten me because the workers only wanted to demonstrate their loyalty to the government. They were looking for something to do; it was like political study. He Da was also criticized.

Each morning at about four o'clock, I got up and went to the Factory to boil water. In the winter, I washed leather in the river. Although I had officially lost my hat, I still experienced active discrimination as a landlord. In the evenings, political meetings were often held, and I had to perform odd jobs, cleaning, and boiling water. I worked hard without holidays.

1 9 6 8

The Cultural Revolution moved into a more violent period when the students started to fight each other with guns. Rumors spread that all the shops would be closed, so people started to stockpile food. I borrowed money from relatives and bought several months' food quota. When the fighting was at its worst, the shops closed for only four days.

1 9 6 9

In August, heavy labor and political meetings quite exhausted me. A rumor about stolen dye material at the Fur and Leather Factory almost caused me to have a nervous breakdown. I was in charge of dyeing the leather. Some workers commented, "So much dye had been used, but there was so little color! Who has stolen the dye material?" I became extremely nervous and was afraid that this allegation would cause me great trouble. I could neither sleep nor eat; my heart beat quickly. I could not recite my *sutras* and almost lost consciousness.

I asked for leave from the Factory; this was granted after the leaders visited my home to confirm that I was really sick. I was granted three months' leave without wages. Although I was seriously sick, I did not have sufficient money to go to the hospital. Shang Yuan's nephew was a Chinese herbal doctor; his treatment saved me.

In late 1969, Lian Di applied to work in the forestry bureau. She had had only one year of primary school. Because the job required strenuous physical labor, few people were interested, especially those from a good family background. She worked in this position for two years in a county in Sichuan Province about three hundred and fifty kilometers from Da Yan, and eventually obtained a position at a steel factory in Kunming.

1 9 7 0

The central government ordered the four types of people to go to the countryside[36] and asked others to go. The Factory leader asked me to fill in a form preparing to go to the countryside. I argued that according to the government documents only class enemies or those with no jobs had to leave; those who could not work did not have to go. As Shang Yuan was still classified as a landlord and had no job, we had to go. Several times the Street Committee warned us that we should leave.

"The earlier one leaves, the better your attitude."

The Street Committee indicated for us to settle down in Qi He, a commune about one hundred and fifty kilometers from Da Yan, near the Yangtze River. My family insisted on not leaving for almost a year; Yi Xing was in the first year of middle school and Qian Di did not want to go.

Yu Ji and Rong Xing were sent to one village where they worked as farmers; Quan Xing and her young family were sent to another village.

Some agitators, who had already settled in the countryside, questioned the Street Committee why my family was still residing in Da Yan. The Street Committee told me that if I did not leave for the countryside my son would not be educated. I was afraid to go to the countryside because my family might not have the opportunity to return to Da Yan and we would become poor farmers. I thought that there would be heavy labor in the countryside; I had never touched farming tools nor experienced farm labor.

Qian Di hid our Da Yan household identification books; she did not want Yi Xing to go with us. I said that it was no use and sent our Da Yan household identification books to the Street Committee. The next day when we received our village household identification books, to our surprise, our ages had been changed. I was one year younger, Qian Di two years older.

According to the government regulations, since Qian Di was now eighteen years old, she could stay in Da Yan. The Street Committee did not agree. Then, she asked them to let Yi Xing stay because he was at the first grade of middle school. "Since the machine was leaving, the screws must leave with it" was the response from the head of the Street Committee. The whole family must move to the countryside.[37]

1 9 7 1

My family celebrated the Qing Ming Festival on April 5th, and swept our ancestors' graves. I was especially sad because I had a feeling that I would never return to Da Yan and that this had been the last Qing Ming Festival. The next day, the Street Committee sent a cadre and two carts to transport us fifteen kilometers to Ji Xiang, a village in the La Shi Commune. The two carts were almost empty as my family had virtually nothing.

The leader of Ji Xiang arranged for us to live in a deserted house. The floors in the house were slanted but overall it was a bit better than the stable.

My family were fortunate that during the first two years in Ji Xiang we received our Da Yan grain and meat quotas. My monthly grain quota was higher (forty *jin*) than the farmers (thirty *jin*). The farmers envied me.

After settling into life in the countryside, I started to recite my *sutras* again in the morning.

1 9 7 2

Because of our improved situation, we had sufficient food for our Spring Festival celebration. Before New Year's Eve we killed a small pig. New Year's Eve was a holiday. I held no ceremony. My family had a large banquet with rice, pork meat, and vegetables. The first two days of Spring Festival were holidays. I held no ceremony. On the second day, I went for a walk by myself to a monastery in a nearby village. The monastery was being used as a school. As there were no classes, it was quiet and peaceful. In the courtyard, I found a plum tree in blossom. Suddenly, a poem came to me:

> *I am a lonely man.*
> *Each year, I become older and older.*
> *The plum blossoms fall petal by petal.*

I feared that I might never return to my home in Da Yan. At that moment, I felt very sad.

I earned ¥20 per month from my work in the village fur and leather shop during 1971-72. Shang Yuan and Qian Di earned another ¥16. People judged you by your work. At the end of the year in the village there was a general distribution. The village accountant balanced the villagers' accounts according to their food quotas and wages. Because I was a handicraftsman doing professional work, I earned the highest wage in the village.

When in the countryside, I got up early each morning to pick up pig droppings on the village road. We had a small vegetable garden; corn grew well. We raised several pigs, ducks, and hencocks. The village leader told others, "These landlords are good at management even in the village. They manage to live well; they are not farmers but they do laboring well."

I had been apprehensive about going to the village because I had no idea about life there. After I was settled, I realized that village life was not as difficult as I had imagined. However, I missed my music and old friends from Da Yan. I was concerned about what had happened to my friends. The villagers envied my family's living condition as it was the best in Ji Xiang. Also, I was free to do what I wanted. During my four years in Ji Xiang, every day with fine weather after supper before sunset, I walked in the fields. While walking, I recited *sutras* and sang music in a low voice.

While we lived in Ji Xiang, all the members of one family (the husband, wife, and daughter) died of pulmonary tuberculosis within two years. The whole village was often haunted. One night, Qian Di and I saw the leader of the village hold an ax in the air. His wife cried and shouted. Nobody was upstairs but they heard a sound from there. Sometimes when spirits appear, there is a wind, and cocks become frightened. I stood outside the front gate and said to myself, "We are not locals. We come from another place. We have no trouble with you. Please do not make trouble with us. Let us take separate roads."

While living in Ji Xiang, I twice asked for permission to visit Da Yan. My first visit was for two days. By visiting my old friends, I realized that my living conditions in Ji Xiang were much better. Although invited by several friends for meals, I did not accept the invitations as I realized that it would be too difficult for them to provide a "good" meal.

1 9 7 3

During April, I made my second two-day visit to Da Yan. Rong Xing, Quan Xing, and Qian Di, and I visited our family graveyard for the Qing Ming Festival. I quietly sat and recited to myself the entire *sutra* book *Opening Prayer*.

Yu Ji, Rong Xing, Quan Xing, and her family returned to Da Yan. All three of them worked at odd jobs earning ¥1 per day. Because their household identification books were still in the village, they could not obtain their grain quotas from the government shop where rice cost ¥0.16 per *jin*. As Lijiang was not a rice growing area, there was no black market for rice in Da Yan; therefore, one of them traveled fifty kilometers to He Qing County to purchase rice at the inflated price of ¥0.70 per *jin*.

My family was told that from then on we should earn our living through our labor and eat our harvest from the village. My main work in Ji Xiang was to teach two apprentices; I was never absent from my work. Shang Yuan tended to the pigs for the brigade. Qian Di labored in the fields while Yi Xing studied at the Commune middle school. After he graduated later that year, he also labored in the fields.

1 9 7 4

In early June, Yang Ru Xin, Rong Xing's fiancé, traveled to Ji Xiang and met with me. He obtained permission to marry my eldest daughter. The wedding day was very simple. Because the groom's parents were dead, there was no ceremony. No firecrackers. However, because there was no active political movement and the situation was freer, they held a ten-table banquet with eight bowls. The next day, I invited the wedding couple and eight family members for supper in Ji Xiang. We served six plates and six bowls.

During these last two years in the village, I developed a special feeling for the country life. The living conditions were good; we had enough food. The local people respected me and treated me well. The village leaders often asked my advice. I had a regular income and was able to use my handicraft skills to serve people. There was no control. I felt free. I did not want to leave. I was concerned that by returning to Da Yan without permission I would be criticized and punished. My family would have no social position, no food supply. I had no courage to return. I had heard of families who had returned under similar conditions, were criticized, and had serious trouble. I did not want any more trouble. Only because Qian Di and Yi Xing could not tolerate country life, I reluctantly agreed to return to Da Yan.

1 9 7 5

In January, the leader of the Ji Xiang Village Committee informed me that he had other plans for the house my family was living in and we must move elsewhere.[38] Because I could not find other accommodation in Ji Xiang, in February, before Spring Festival, my family and I secretly left Ji Xiang and returned, without permission, to Da Yan. Both the village leader and the Da Yan Street Committee knew but did not question us. We returned to the stable. During our four year absence, I had loaned it to a relative, who was our neighbor.

I went to the Street Committee to ask them for a job. Since I had been employed at the Fur and Leather Factory before going to Ji Xiang, I was told that I must ask them for a job. The factory official told me that he would give me a job if I could show him my Da Yan household identification book. As I was still registered officially as living in Ji Xiang, in the La Shi Commune, my household identification book was there. No book — no job.

I returned to the Street Committee and requested them to transfer my household identification book from the La Shi Commune back to Da Yan. They refused because there was no clear document from the central government stating that landlords could return from the villages. The Street Committee did not want to open the door just for me. Thus, I could not obtain a formal position.

Without our household identification books, my family and I could only work at odd jobs. Also, no household identification books meant no access to the government grain shops. Therefore, Qian Di traveled fifty kilometers to He Qing County to buy rice on the black market.

From before Spring Festival, I stayed at home and people, who knew that I had returned, brought coats and quilts to be repaired with scraps of leather. Shang Yuan did a small business as a peddler buying hens and eggs in a village and selling them in the market. Yi Xing and Qian Di worked at odd jobs. Sometimes, my relatives, who had not used their full monthly quotas, lent us their food certificates so we could buy food in the government shops.

After returning to Da Yan, almost every morning after reciting my *sutras* I did several minutes of *qigong*. I possessed a strong desire to live. My life started to proceed smoothly and I did not worry.

1 9 7 6

In September, Mao Tse Tung died. In December, the Gang of Four was put down.

1 9 7 7

Early in the year, normal college entrance examinations were reinstated. Applicants were accepted for college according to their marks. Yi Xing passed the entrance examination for a technical college in Kunming. To attend the college, he required a Da Yan household identification book; his book was still in Ji Xiang. Qian Di traveled to Ji Xiang and asked permission from the village leader to transfer Yi Xing's household identification book back to Da Yan. He refused.

Qian Di returned to Da Yan and met with the leaders of the Lijiang County Education Bureau. She argued that Yi Xing had passed the entrance examination and should be allowed to attend the technical college in Kunming. The leaders agreed and organized for Yi Xing's household identification book to be returned to Da Yan and he was able to attend to the Kunming technical college.

As there was no tuition fee, Yi Xing's expenses were textbooks and his room and board. While in Ji Xiang, I had saved ¥60 which I gave to Yi Xing towards his school expenses. The college was near Lian Di's unit in Kunming, the steel company; he was able to live with her. Before 1975, the Street Committee undertook to employ, in a United Factory, the many jobless who had not gone to the countryside. Carpenters, cobblers, and handicraftsmen worked in separate shops. When people started returning from the countryside, they could join the United Factory.

That summer, an older Tibetan woman went to the Street Committee and asked for a job. She had worked at odd jobs at the Fur and Leather Factory and knew me. She wanted to start a handicrafts business and discussed this with me before suggesting that she could work together with Shang Yuan and myself. After a lot of trouble, the Tibetan lady, Shang Yuan, an apprentice, and myself established a small shop. We sold Naxi capes (¥30) and long, leather coats (¥50). Each day after work, an accountant from the United Factory came and took our daily earnings and distributed them. Shang Yuan and I each received ¥24 a month.

At this time, I was pleased that Shang Yuan and I had jobs, Yi Xing was going to school, and our living conditions had improved greatly. We could purchase our grains at the average price in government shops and lived reasonably well.

All my friends before liberation had been landlords; since liberation, society had always looked down upon us. Among all the former Da Yan landlord families, my son was the first to pass a college entrance examination and go to a technical college in Kunming. Some families commented Yi Xing had a last opportunity, "to pick a moon from the sea;" others could not understand how I allowed my son to attend a technical college and study to become a bus driver. I responded that any education was better than no education. Yi Xing had no other educational possibility.

From this year, because there was a freer atmosphere after the Gang of Four, I resumed making an offering to my ancestors at Spring Festival and at the Qing Ming Festival, almost as before liberation. For the Qing Ming Festival, I visited my fami-

ly graveyard for a memorial service and made offerings to my
parents and ancestors. I often sat in front of my parents' tomb
thinking profoundly. Each year on the anniversaries of my parents' deaths, good vegetarian meals were prepared to commemorate them.

1 9 7 8

I was very relieved. A ray of light suddenly appeared in the
cloudy sky. This gave me a little hope for the future. The Street
Committee did the necessary paperwork to transfer my family's
household identification books from the La Shi Commune back
to Da Yan. Yu Ji, Rong Xing, and Quan Xing also received their
household identification books. Since all our household identification books were now registered in Da Yan, we all had access
to our grain quotas at the government shops.

In December, there was an important meeting of the
Communist Party in Beijing. Before this Congress the main task
of the Party had been class struggle; after this Congress, the
main target of the Party was economic construction. The Party
started to reform the over-concentration of political power and
economic management. They invited foreign enterprises to
invest in China. Before there had been only state-owned units;
now, a private person could conduct his own business, be self-
employed.

The Communist Party considered 1949 the first liberation;
however, it was followed by a series of political movements
which classified people and jailed many of them. The 1978 document was considered a second liberation for many people. The
"four types of people" classification was discarded. Everybody

was considered a normal person. Those who had been forced to move to the countryside could return to their original residences. Shang Yuan was no longer classified as a landlord.

1 9 7 9

In December, Yi Xing married a Han woman. There was no ceremony, no music, no firecrackers. I invited forty tables. My friends brought gifts and were served a lunch of six bowls and six plates. After lunch they went home. For supper, I invited twenty tables; my friends brought gifts and were served a supper of six bowls and six plates.

1 9 8 1

When I learned that my daughter-in-law was pregnant, the next morning I prayed to Wen Chang to send me a grandson.

1 9 8 2

The leaders of the Street Committee told me about a new policy from the central government of "contracting with responsibility."[39] The United Factory was closed. Shang Yuan and I did not want to continue working with the Tibetan lady. The Street Committee said that we had worked together for five years and were familiar with one another. Also, how could the Tibetan woman manage without us? So, Shang Yuan, the Tibetan woman, and I contracted with the Street Committee to run our small shop. We each earned more than ¥30 per month.

The Street Committee returned the ¥1000 to Yu Ji that the
Red Guards had confiscated in 1967 during the Cultural
Revolution.

Before this year, I felt that the Street Committee held me by
my neck, I did not feel free. Everything was controlled by and
depended upon the Street Committee. Now with this new policy,
my living condition became much better. I felt quite content with
my life. I could breathe freely.

In August, my prayers were answered with the birth of my
grandson. One month later, without a ceremony, I named him
Hong Lu and invited some friends for supper.

1 9 8 3

Shang Yuan, the Tibetan lady, and I became self-employed
and no longer paid the contract fee to the Street Committee.
Since being self-employed, we together earned over ¥200 per
month. I felt much better being self-employed. Work more, earn
more. Year by year, we saved more capital to purchase the items
we wanted.

1 9 8 4

My family celebration of Spring Festival was much better
than in Ji Xiang. Even though we had money in Ji Xiang, the village shops carried a very limited selection of goods. Shang Yuan,
Yi Xing, his wife, and I celebrated New Year's Eve together in the
stable. We held a short ceremony during which we burnt *joss*
sticks, knelt down, and made offerings. We enjoyed a large meal,

including a boiled, salted, pig's head; the meal was almost as extensive as before liberation.

To avoid criticism, I followed the fashion with the new holidays and Festivals (March 8th (1952), Women's Day; May 1st (1950), May (Labor) Day; June 1st (1955), Children's Day; July 1st (1950), founding of the Chinese Communist Party; August 1st (1950), founding of the People's Liberation Army; September 10th (1986), Teachers' Day; October 1st (1950), National Day, founding of the People's Republic of China). I boiled a piece of meat and ate a good supper, but all had no meaning for me.

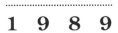

1 9 8 8

We purchased a washing machine, a rice cooker, a tape recorder, and a television.

1 9 8 9

The Tibetan lady volunteered to leave the shop; Shang Yuan and I gave her one-third of the shop's capital and she started her own business.

1 9 9 0

In July, special paper boards were sold in the street. Shang Yuan purchased one. For the first time since 1948, I celebrated the Festival of Accepting and Sending Back Ancestral Spirits. On July 10th, for accepting our ancestral spirits, I placed the paper board on a table. Shang Yuan prepared two bowls of noodles and placed one on either side of the paper board. I lit *joss* sticks and a pair of candles. The candles were placed on either side of the paper board. My family bowed, then knelt before the paper board, and we said to ourselves, "The souls of our ancestors have come, treat them well."

A little food was placed outside the front gate to ward off bad spirits. We ate an early vegetarian supper on July 14th. For sending back our ancestral spirits, we placed paper clothes and money in a paper bag and burnt it; the ashes were placed in a basin and thrown into river.

Before liberation, even young men wanted to participate in the rite; today, young men do not understand the significance, are not interested — a lost tradition.

1 9 9 2

My day started at six o'clock when I awoke. After thirty minutes of reciting *sutras* while practicing *qigong* in bed, I got up and joined Shang Yuan for a breakfast of *baba* and Tibetan tea. Around eight o'clock, we walked to our shop and prepared for the day's work. At twelve o'clock we had lunch; we either brought food from home, or purchased some rice noodles, and ate in the shop. After lunch, Shang Yuan remained in the shop and I walked to a friend's house to play cards. I returned to the shop at five o'clock. After closing the shop, we walked home. We stopped in the market and purchased some meat. For our supper, we prepared meat, vegetables, and rice. Sometimes on the weekends, Yi Xing, his wife, and my two grandsons joined us for a meal. In the evenings, sometimes there was an orchestra concert; if there was no concert, I usually stayed at home and watched television. At nine o'clock, I retired.

The reforms of December, 1978 gave local people permission to celebrate their festivals publicly. Because Da Yan is in such an isolated region, it was only in 1983 that the local government required a Naxi orchestra to provide entertainment at a public function.

Before this time, *Dongjing* music was played privately. Initially, I did not join the orchestra because I was afraid that some common people may make gossip and say bad words about me. "Even a landlord can sit and play music publicly in the park." Then, I might be punished. Several years later before the 1985 Spring Festival, I was invited to join the orchestra to play

He Yi An playing cards.

the ten gongs and give proper direction. I felt very happy, almost as if in a dream. Could I have other better days in the future?

I had not touched the instruments for twenty-three years. I had thought that I would never touch the instruments again. The first piece we played was *Spring has Come*. From that performance in 1985 until last night, when we played *Qing He Lao Ren*, I felt as if Wen Chang appeared before me in my mind. The piece of music describes an old man sitting by a calm stream who obtained truth from Daoism, understood Daoism.

The three volumes of the Da Dong Xian Jing are very precious[40]
The sutras are more splendid than jewels and gold
The sutras assist people to overcome disasters, avoid troubles,
and have a new life
Through long-term sutra study, even evildoers can
become good persons

The sutras appeared while the great Dao was spreading on earth
You will obtain great rewards if you help people and
do good deeds
If a human being wants to live in heaven
He must make his mind calm and quiet and then study
the wonderful sutras

There is no soft breeze nor white clouds over the sea
The air and sky are calm and quiet
If you no longer have earthly desires
Your life will become calm, quiet, and eternal

The proper time for reciting sutras is on lucky days[41]
There is nothing on earth to disturb your mind
The right way to success is always to give your heart
to helping others
Thus your name will be inscribed on the jade list in the
golden book of heaven
Human beings are pure and innocent, when they come
to this earth they have nothing
Only great persons never delight in sensual pleasures
Excellent persons prefer to do the most difficult things
Gods in heaven are very intelligent and reward people according
to their actions

He Yi An playing the Ten Gongs and
Tibetan Prayer Bell.

The next morning I awoke at six o'clock and sat up on my bed. I crossed my legs, closed my eyes, breathed calmly, and recited quietly to myself for thirty minutes the *sutra* book *Opening Prayer*. In my mind, I thought about the *sutra*, pronounced it correctly, and stood respectfully beside Wen Chang.

C L O S I N G   P R A Y E R

Since He Yi An repeatedly stressed the importance of his ancestors during our interviews, I suggested that we visit his family graveyard. He Yi An responded favorably to my suggestion and agreed to make the necessary arrangements for the excursion.

On November 26th, 1991, He Yi An, Lu Feng, and myself, were driven in a Chinese Cherokee Jeep to the outskirts of a village about eight kilometers outside Da Yan. He Yi An brought a thermos with boiled water, tea, glasses, *baba*, and biscuits. Lu Feng brought tangerines, biscuits, and six small fruit drink cartons. I brought my camera equipment. After a short discussion, He Yi An allowed us to carry his thermos and refreshments.

He Yi An led us along the edges of the fields until we reached the base of the mountain. Eighty years ago along this same route, his stepmother carried young He Yi An on her back to the family graveyard for the Qing Ming Festival. As we started our ascent, I thought of how many times He Yi An had followed this route during his lifetime. After climbing for about twenty minutes, we stopped for a rest. Lu Feng gave us each a tangerine. As we climbed higher, it became quieter and the smell of pine cones filled the air. After a further sixty minutes of climbing, we reached a flatter region. I assumed that we were approaching the graveyard. A ten-minute walk brought us there.

It was so peaceful, so quiet, so calm. Walking into the clearing, I saw a large number of tombs. Ten generations of He Yi An's family were buried here.

Walking closer, we saw neat mounds of freshly dug soil on the left side of most of the tombs. The bones of his ancestors were scattered on the ground in front of the tombs. The graves had been robbed!

The freshness of the dug soil indicated that the thieves' visit preceded ours by just several days. They had dug precisely at the position of the women's skulls and had stolen their jade earrings. A pair of antique jade earrings fetch ¥2000 to ¥3000. He Yi An was noticeably shaken. Lu Feng and I were shocked. We looked at each other in amazement. This possibility had never entered my mind. How would He Yi An respond?

As a dutiful son, his first action was to collect some pine branches and sweep in front of his parents' tomb. After placing the pine branches in front of the tomb, with a distraught expression on his face, he sat there motionless. He was crying.

He Yi An at his parents' grave.

After a time, he walked slowly around to the back of the tomb. He stared, with an unbelieving look on his face, at the hole in the ground by his mother's side of his parents' tomb. Her skull was visible. After standing there motionless for several minutes, he picked up some of the black painted coffin wood and threw it back into the grave.

"Mama," he spoke quietly. "Do not worry. I shall fix everything."

The traditional green dragon and white tiger no longer provided adequate protection for the family graveyard.

After a time, we sat and took some refreshment. I thought of the many happy times He Yi An had sat in this very spot with his parents and taken refreshment. We drank tea and ate *baba*. He poured fresh water into our glasses and spoke softly.

"To steal from the living is one thing. From the dead is another. Before, traditionally, everyone respected the sanctity of ancestors. No one would touch a blade of grass in another's family graveyard. Today, this respect does not exist."

Sitting with He Yi An in his family graveyard, he must have been thinking about his whole life because it flashed through my mind. I looked at him and thought. Some moments, I believe that He Yi An is an elusive water dragon, changing his forms, his actions, in the mist.

Other moments, I believe that He Yi An is, in fact, Wen Chang.

The great Dao is not very far away[42]
The great Dao is in your mind
Everything will have an end at last

But your life is eternal
If you continue to cultivate your body and mind
Your life will be continuously refreshed
Once you have mastered the essence of the Dao
You will enjoy eternal life

APPENDIX

1. DONGJING SOCIETY ACTIVITIES:
WEN CHANG AND GENERAL GUAN GATHERINGS

The timing of the February and August Wen Chang gatherings of the *Dongjing* Society imitated the Confucian tradition of being in a "good season." The February 3rd gathering was to admire Wen Chang and celebrate his birthday. These sentiments were read by the leader of the Society from red characters written on a yellow paper; the paper was placed, with paper money, in a yellow envelope and burnt in a candle flame. This symbolized posting a letter to the gods.

The August 3rd gathering was to give thanks to Wen Chang, especially by those successful candidates from the government examinations. Gatherings started two days before the day to be celebrated. At the two Wen Chang gatherings, the *Da Dong Xian Jing* was recited. The essence of the *Da Dong Xian Jing*, the five books, is contained in three volumes with twenty-four chapters.

Volume One outlined ten disciplines for each gathering: 1. The statue of Wen Chang displayed in the center of the main table. 2. On the main table, three-legged pots placed to hold lit *joss* sticks. 3. Not to sleep with their wives. 4. Not to eat meat. 5. Wear clean clothes, dress correctly. 6. Give up worldly desires. 7. Purify mind, maintain calm heart. 8. Recite *sutras,* pronouncing the characters correctly. 9. Recite *sutras,* chanting according to the notation. 10. Study and practice politeness and good behavior.

The *Dongjing* Society gatherings took place over five days. The first day was for preparations with no ceremonies. The *Dongjing* Society was divided into four groups; each group was responsible for the management of one gathering. Two knowledgeable members were selected as assistants for a gathering to recite *sutras* and assist with the ceremonies. Younger members cleaned the temple and set up the tables and chairs. Red silk with a *baqua* symbol covered the eight main tables. In front of the long table, there was a square table covered with red silk with the I Ching symbol. Long, colored silk banners, each with one of Wen Chang's twenty titles, plus a hanging scroll with Sanduo's name, were displayed on the walls. Some members were responsible for purchasing vegetables in the market.

Six members went to collect the statues of Wen Chang, Tian Long, the Heaven Deaf God who holds a book about Wen Chang's good deeds and his descendants, and Di Ya, the Earth Dumb God who carries a jade decoration for good luck. They were transported to the temple on copper plates accompanied by other members carrying lit *joss* sticks. The statues were placed on the main table, the taller Wen Chang statue in the center, Tian Long on the left, and Di Ya on the right. A three-legged *joss* stick pot stood in front of each statue. Tian Long and Di Ya were students of Wen Chang who became immortals. These two smaller statues accentuated the significance of Wen Chang. At the left end of the table, *Yuan Chen Shan Guo, Having Obtained Good Merits and Virtues,* was placed; this book contained the names of all the deceased members. At the right end of the table, *Yong Bao Ping An* or *Safety Forever,* was placed; this book contained the names of all current members.

If you understand Daoism yourself,
god will give you a reward.
Why burn joss sticks?
gods live in heaven;
air floats to heaven,
air informs gods;
gods come by air.
Recite sutras before joss sticks,
use pure water to wash head and hands.
The left hand holds a book,
the right hand a sword,
then recite the following incantations:
body purification,
mind purification,
mouth purification,
heaven and earth purification,
for gods living under earth, and golden lights.
Then, the ceremony starts.

The temple opened at daybreak on the second day. After the sound of the gong, the members lit *joss* sticks. After the drum was hit, in groups of three from the eldest to the youngest, the members started to enter the temple and bowed down in front of Wen Chang. When all the members were seated at the tables, the leader announced that a new gathering had started and read the Invocation:

We are created as dignified men
The profound meaning of the Dao is elusive
If during our whole life we sincerely devote ourselves
to Wen Chang

Surely Wen Chang will understand us and reward us
Today we shall start a gathering to explain the
mysteries of the sutras
First, we must demonstrate our sincerity to Wen Chang
To accomplish this, we have burnt fragrant joss sticks
Now, we shall recite the sutras loudly and perfectly

The members then chanted the response:
Today, at this gathering we are reciting the sutras together
At first, we shall do our utmost to pray for our country
We have informed heaven and the gods who will be present
Fragrant joss sticks are burning in the jade burners
If the Emperor's political power is solid and the whole
country is united
The great Dao will be as prosperous as the sun and moon
People will live and work in peace and contentment
We wish we could have a good harvest, peace, and
tranquillity each year.

The group then completed reciting the *sutra* book *Opening Prayer*.

For breakfast, they were served steamed buns and drank Tibetan tea. After breakfast, they started to recite, with music, the invitation ceremony inviting the gods to come; one poem for each of the more than forty gods. After about two hours, they had lunch. For lunch, they were served four bowls, and four dishes, all vegetable (fried bean curd, fried potato, other vegetables, and rice). Each table had a plate of butter to mix with the rice. After lunch the gong sounded, they reassembled and completed the invitation ceremony.

After performing the music for *Bagua* and chanting four poems, these four poems were different from those when *Bagua* was used as accompaniment for reciting the three volumes of the *Da Dong Xian Jing*, they demonstrated their respect to the gods by performing *Ten Offerings*. The ceremony entailed a spoken explanation of the offering, playing a musical piece while the item was offered, and then chanting *Ten Offerings* with the musical accompaniment after each of the ten offerings. The first offering was flowers and the musical piece *Everlasting Flowers;* the second fruit with *Dai Wu;* the third incense with *Waves Washing the Sand;* the fourth rice with *Man Wu Yan;* the fifth tea with *Spring Has Come*; the sixth clothes with *Summer Has Come;* the seventh water with *Song of a Water Dragon;* the eighth Daoist talismans with *Autumn Has Come;* the ninth lamp and wine with *Winter Has Come;* the tenth jewels with *Swaying Willow Leaves.*

This was followed by chanting the first book of the *Da Dong Xian Jing*. The orchestra played *Primordial Heavenly King* while the members chanted the first poem of *Primordial Heavenly King*. The assistant on the left recited the first chapter of the first volume of the *Da Dong Xian Jing*. While the assistant was reciting, the other members either listened or followed in their *sutra* books. The orchestra played *Bagua* while the members chanted the first poem of *Bagua*. Then, the orchestra repeated *Primordial Heavenly King* while the members chanted the second poem. The assistant on the right recited the second chapter of the first volume. The orchestra repeated *Bagua* while the members chanted the second poem. This procedure was followed for the remaining six chapters. Around four o'clock, they had a break for tea and rice cakes.

After the break, they completed the first volume and all the members stood. The older members moved to form two lines facing each other perpendicular to the center table; the middle-aged members stood behind them. The younger members stood facing the statues, knelt down once to acknowledge their appreciation and thanks to their masters, the older members. The old members acknowledged by bowing. For supper, they were served six bowls, and four dishes, all vegetable. After supper, the members went home.

On the third day they followed the same procedure for entering the temple. After completing the opening ceremony, they offered a series of special gifts to Wen Chang to convince him of their sincerity. For this ceremony, the leader knelt in front of Wen Chang and the orchestra played *Goats on the Hill.* One assistant handed the kneeling leader an offering from the right. The leader held the offering in front of Wen Chang and then passed it to the other assistant on the left. Then, the offering was placed on the center table. The following items were presented as offerings: first a cup of tea, second a cup of liquor, third a cup of date juice, fourth a plate with a peach, fifth a plate with a deer leg, sixth a piece of silk embroidered with dragon and phoenix patterns. The first five offerings were repeated for a second time with the sixth a plate with fruits, honey, and olives. The first five offerings were repeated for a third time with the sixth a basket of rice. Another member came forward and read a poem written in red characters on a yellow piece of paper explaining the reason for the gathering. By reciting the *Da Dong Xian Jing,* the members cultivated themselves; by reciting the *Incantation Book,* they obtained magical powers to call the gods to drive away evil spirits. This yellow paper was given to the leader who placed it in an envelope with paper money. While the orchestra played *Wind Blowing Along the River,* the leader and one of the assistants went out into the courtyard and burnt the envelope in a candle flame. This was followed by reciting the second volume of the *Da Dong Xian Jing* with the *Primordial Heavenly King* and *Bagua* accompaniment. Then, the younger members acknowledged their masters. The group then completed the third volume of the *Da Dong Xian Jing*; the younger members again acknowledged their masters. Meals were served at appropriate times.

On the fourth day, they followed the same entrance procedure and recited the *sutra* book *Opening Prayer*. They proceeded to chant the *Incantation Book* while playing the piece *Incantation*. The musical tempos and volume fluctuated greatly. After completing the *Incantation Book,* the orchestra played *Qing He Lao Ren,* the name of an old Daoist who after mastering the *Da Dong Xian Jing* wrote fourteen poems to admire the *sutras,* while the members chanted the fourteen accompanying poems. Once *Qing He Lao Ren* was completed, candles were lit, placed in the temple, and *Deng ke* was performed. The two assistants knelt down at either end of the main, center table. The assistant on the left recited two poems, then the group responded with two poems while beating the drums and hitting the gongs and cymbals. Then, the assistant on the right recited two poems, the group responded with two poems while beating the drums and hitting the gongs and cymbals. When they completed the *Deng ke* book, the leader read the conclusion from a yellow paper.

"We invited the gods from heaven for three days. With the gods' help, we finished three days of study. Now, we have obtained magical powers from the Incantation Book. We thank the gods. We now send the gods back to heaven."

After the conclusion, all members left the temple and ordered themselves according to their ages. In groups of three, starting with the eldest, they entered the temple. Each group knelt down in front of the statues, nodded their heads three times, stood up, left the temple and were free to return home.

On the fifth day, there was no ceremony. For breakfast, they were served meat. They spent the morning socializing, playing cards, and resting. For lunch, they were served a banquet. Eight members sat at each table, the older ones in the temple, the middle aged just outside, and the youngest in the courtyard. They drank liquor and each table was served a steamed, salted pig's head. After lunch, there was free time. For supper, six bowls, and four dishes, mainly meat, were served. After supper, the statues were sent back to scholars' homes and the younger members collected the decorations, *sutra* books, copper plates, and placed them in large wooden boxes which were stored at a merchant's house.

In May and June, the *Dongjing* Society held gatherings to honor General Guan Yu. On May 13th, General Guan Yu exhibited extreme courage and bravery by going alone to eat at an enemy's banquet; thus, the May gathering paid tribute to the General's personal loyalty and bravery. General Guan's birthday was June 24th; thus, the June gathering celebrated his birthday.

The General Guan gatherings were held in a different temple, different statues worshiped, and different *sutras* recited. Otherwise, they followed the five-day format of the Wen Chang gatherings. On the center table in the General Guan temple, the statue of General Guan Yu was placed in the center; to the left was that of his son, Guan Ping, holding his father's seal; and to the right was that of General Zhou Cang, a follower of General Guan, holding General Guan's scimitar. The *Enlightenment Sutras* were recited. The statues were kept by the Clan Mu.

Besides the four official gatherings, the *Dongjing* Society participated in members', or members' family, funerals by holding a ceremony in which they chanted *sutras* and played music. Also, for members they performed three ceremonies. The first was for the third anniversary of a parent's death and the second to pass safely the unlucky 36th and 49th years. For both of these ceremonies, they performed the Rite of Lighting a Candle and Making a Wish and recited *Deng ke*. For the first ceremony, the wish expressed the children's gratitude to the parent who had taken care of them. For the second ceremony, the wish was for the gods to bless the member with good luck to pass safely the bad year. The third ceremony was for a new house.

To select the correct location for the house, the person consulted a geomancer. He determined which of the twenty-four soil veins the house should be built on to guarantee its safety. Once the house was completed, the owner invited his friends and members of the *Dongjing* Society to a banquet. In the center of the courtyard, a hole was dug and a pot placed in it. The pot was filled with spring water from five different sources. A silver or gold shaped fish and swallow (representing treasure and good luck) were placed in the pot and it was covered with a stone. An invited *Dongjing* Society member, who would be chanting the *sutra*, threw five types of seeds (rice, corn, bean, wheat, and oats) around the pot. This ceremony signified that the house was built on treasure and that the family would be wealthy and prosperous. The members of the *Dongjing* Society then recited the special Wen Chang *sutra*– *An Long Dian Tu Ke Yi, Rite for Pacification of the Dragon and Settling of the Earth,* or *Rite for Discovering a Correct Soil Vein and Locating a House on a Good Site.*

The expenditure for a five day *Dongjing* Society gathering was one hundred and twenty silver dollars. For each gathering, usually seventy to eighty members attended and each contributed two silver dollars; rent income from the Society's properties covered any shortfall. Each gathering had twenty hosts who handled the organization of the event. For the ceremonies for the Society's members, no fees were charged but the host family provided meals for the participating members.

For those who did not belong to the *Dongjing* Society, Daoist priests were available for these and other ceremonies. In Da Yan, there were ten professional Daoist priests. After a ceremony, the priest usually attached pieces of paper with incantations on them to the pillars of the main gate to protect the family from evil ghosts.

THE RITE OF LIGHTING A CANDLE AND MAKING A WISH

Members performed this rite, before or after lunch, during the third ceremonial day of a gathering. For the rite, he took a plate of rice and a string of fifty copper coins, two boxes of sugar, paper money, *joss* sticks, and a pair of candles to the temple. He gave these items to the family who took care of the temple. Before the ceremony, at a table outside the temple, a member, skilled in calligraphy, wrote the wishes in red ink on a piece of yellow paper.

Before lunch, the ceremony started in the temple. The two members, or assistants, in charge were called 'lamp watchers' and were young or middle-aged members who had good voices and could read all the poems. They stood on either side of the main, center table. The assistant on the left announced, "Now beat the drum and start the ceremony."

The drum was beaten. Those performing the rite thrice placed lit *joss* sticks in the pot. On the center table there were three statues; from left to right, Tian Long, the Heaven Deaf god; Wen Chang, the god of literature; and Di Ya, the Earth Dumb god. Three candles stood in front of these statues; the left one represented good fortune, the center one wealth, and the right one longevity. The candles were in stands surrounded by circles of rice with a thread of rice joining the three circles. On the table, in front of the three candles, there were four Chinese characters for good fortune, wealth, longevity, and heirs, formed with rice. To the left of the center table, seven candles represented the seven stars of the Big Dipper, the north. To the right of the center table, six candles represented the six stars of The Archer, the south. On the ground in front of the center table, there was a single candle in a holder on a plate full of rice; this candle was for the people performing the rite. After the people lit all the candles, they knelt down and held their yellow wish papers over their heads.

The ceremony started with the assistant on the left reciting two poems from *Deng ke, Lighting a Candle for Driving Away Disasters and Avoiding Trouble;* a Daoist book used for this rite. The members replied with two poems. The assistant on the right then recited two poems; the members replied with two poems. When the ceremony was completed, those performing the rite stood, walked in front of the center candle and burnt their yellow wish papers, sending their wishes to heaven.

2. QING MING FESTIVAL

Qing Ming was a festival to pay respect to one's ancestors. The date was usually March 5th. Food was prepared on March 4th. Early the next morning after He Ru Lin finished reciting his *sutras,* they departed for the family graveyard. Before climbing the hills to the graveyard, a tea kettle was filled with water. After a ninety minute climb, they reached the graveyard. Sticks were gathered, a fire lit, and water boiled for tea. Then, they knelt down in front of a stone which protected the tombs when the family was away. An offering was made to the stone by pouring a cup of tea water and a cup of liquor on the ground in front of it. *Joss* sticks were burnt and firecrackers lit off. Starting with the oldest ancestor, three lit *joss* sticks were placed on the tomb and then the family knelt down and recited a prayer.

"Qing Ming Festival has come. The family has come to be with you."

In front of the tomb an offering was made by pouring some tea water and some liquor. The family then performed the same ritual in front of each tomb in descending order of the ancestors' age. After completing this ceremony, the family sat in a circle with his parents' backs to tombs and ate their meal. For most families it was a happy occasion, a family outing, green fields, breathing fresh air, a picnic. Only if there had been a recent death was the family sad.

3. FESTIVAL OF ACCEPTING AND SENDING BACK ANCESTRAL SPIRITS

On July 10th, in the morning, grandmother, the senior female family member, prepared two bowls of noodles and placed them at the front gate for several minutes. Noodles were a sign of welcome. Then, she returned into the courtyard with the two bowls of noodles and threw pine needles to pave a clean path for the spirits. She then proceeded to enter the downstairs main room and placed a bowl of noodles on either side of a paper board inscribed with the names of the He family ancestors. He Ru Lin exchanged pure water, lit *joss* sticks, lit a pair of candles and an oil lamp. The candles were placed on either side of the paper board and the lamp beside it. Since the souls of their ancestors lived in darkness, the light assisted them to recognize the house and family. Then, the family faced the wooden board, knelt down and said to themselves, "The souls of our ancestors have come, treat them well."

They made an offering by pouring tea water and liquor in front of the board, followed by placing a bowl of rice and several other bowls of food in front of the board. Grandmother took a bowl with pure water and with a pair of chopsticks took some noodles and other food from the other offering bowls and placed them into the bowl with the pure water. She carried this bowl outside the gate and poured its contents onto the ground; this offering was for the bad ghosts, or devils, from those who did not have a natural death (suicide, drowning, or died young). They did not want their spirits to enter the house.

On July 13th, in the evening, they had a good supper, eight bowls, meat and vegetables; the last supper that year with their ancestors. On July 14th, they had an early supper (vegetables only) between three and four o'clock. The early supper was to ensure that their ancestors' spirits would have adequate time to return to heaven that day.

After supper, they knelt down in front of the wooden board for the last ceremony of sending clothes and money to heaven with their ancestral spirits. Paper clothes and money, in the form of silver paper, were placed in a paper bag and burnt. The ashes were thrown into the river, symbolizing sending these items to heaven with their ancestors. Chinese herbs and porridge were boiled, the mixture was taken out to the street and thrown on the road to satiate the hunger of ghosts and devils in the hills.

4. NEW YEAR'S EVE

New Year's Eve was the whole day before the first day of Spring Festival. A square table was placed in the center of the courtyard. Four to five pieces of woven bamboo sheet were used to form a box with one opening; the box was decorated with pine tree needles and a one meter pine tree positioned in the center. This structure was called the "tent of heaven and earth", also called "the pine tent." Pine is a symbol of heaven.

A basket with rice, salt, sugar and tea was placed in the tent as an offering to heaven. Several clean stones were collected from the river bed and placed in the oven; *Artemisia*, wormwood, was picked and placed in a copper pot; the hot stones were placed on the plant. A little vinegar was sprinkled on the stones; the vinegar vaporized producing a good smell in courtyard.

He Ru Lin wore a new, blue, long mandarin jacket; He Yi An a black silk jacket; Huang Qi Zhen her Han clothes, jade earrings, and a gold bracelet. Only before Spring Festival did children receive new clothes. Around three o'clock in the afternoon, He Ru Lin led his family to light *joss* sticks, kneel down three times in front of the "tent of heaven and earth" for the start of the sacrifice to heaven ceremony. A year had passed. God had granted them a good year. They hoped that the coming year would be a good year. He Ru Lin then led the family upstairs to continue the ceremony.

The whole family entered the chapel and their offering of a boiled, salted pig's head and a cock were placed in front of the statues of Xuan Tian, Guan Yin, and Wen Chang. He Yi An exchanged pure water and lit *joss* sticks. The whole family knelt down; He Ru Lin and He Yi An recited the *sutra* book *Opening Prayer*.

The family then went into the left room and knelt down in front of the statue of Zhao Gong Ming, the god of wealth. The family returned downstairs into courtyard and knelt down facing east (loyalty), north (to Sanduo, the local Naxi holy ancestor), the main room (earth), and, finally, the park (the dragon).

The family went to the river and bowed with their offering for the god of water. They poured tea water and liquor and dropped some small pieces of food into the water.

The family made a similar offering to the god of the gate. The pig's head and cock were cut into pieces; this offering was carried upstairs into the room containing the wooden boards with the names of the family members carved into them, and placed in front of the boards and the family knelt down for the ancestors' ceremony. They prayed that their ancestors would bless them with a good year. They returned downstairs and had supper. After supper, the adults sat in chairs, He Yi An knelt down before his elders; the adults gave him pocket money, "red money." Before going to sleep, everyone would bathe to wash away the dirt from last year. They washed their faces and feet, or took a bath if possible.

5. SPRING FESTIVAL

On the first day of Spring Festival at daybreak, He Yi An got up and lit three *joss* sticks, went to the well in the courtyard, fetched pure water and left the lit *joss* sticks by the well. He entered the chapel, exchanged pure water, and lit four one-meter, decorated *joss* sticks. Back in the courtyard in front of the "tent of heaven and earth," the family in a simple ceremony made the sacrifice to heaven and earth with an offering of honey-sweetened Chinese olives and twelve sticky rice cakes. This offering was carried upstairs and the ceremony repeated in each of the three rooms.

For breakfast, they had sticky rice cakes and tea; twelve rice cakes were prepared, each one represented a month of the year. For lunch and supper, they ate vegetables and rice (mixed with butter), bean curd, small black mushrooms, and beans. In the "tent of heaven and earth," they placed a basket containing rice, a parcel of tea, sugar, and salt, for the sacrifice to the heaven ceremony. Women were not allowed out of the house on this first day as they would bring back dirt. During the evening from first to fifth days of Spring Festival, all the family played "hunting," a Chinese dice game.

On the second day, He Yi An got up, exchanged pure water, and knelt down before the wooden boards with his ancestors' names in the upstairs family room. For breakfast, broth was used to prepare the rice; the family ate meat for lunch and supper. In the evening, red lanterns were hung in the courtyard and firecrackers lit off.

On the third day, after breakfast, the whole family walked for ninety minutes to visit the family graveyard. They carried tea, sweets, and cake. Upon arrival, they burnt *joss* sticks and knelt down to the god of the hill (a stone). Lit *joss* sticks were placed on each tomb followed by an offering. They took refreshment before returning home.

On the fourth and fifth days, they visited friends' homes. In the evening, young men met in the Black Dragon Park by the pond, lit off firecrackers and started a dragon dance. They danced through the streets and stopped in front of shops or wealthy families, danced, and received money.

On the sixth day, they repeated the ceremonies and offerings of the first day. The "tent of heaven and earth" was dismantled as the family ceremonial days of Spring Festival were over.

On the eleventh day, the Clan Mu invited a *dongba* to perform a sacrifice to heaven ceremony in their family temple. After the Clan Mu ceremony, ordinary people held their ceremonies.

Most families in Da Yan stopped practicing this ceremony after the Muslim uprising (1875).

Starting on the 14th day of Spring Festival, "Shang Yuan Hui" was celebrated. This "Heaven Gathering" was to congratulate the gods in heaven to have a good year. Over three days, a large ceremony was held at the Grand Monastery in Da Yan. From the five *Karmapa* (Red) Sect monasteries outside of Da Yan, seventy to eighty lamas participated in chanting *sutras* for a good year, a healthy year, and a prosperous year.

Merchants from twenty shops in Da Yan invited the *Dongjing* Society to perform for three days reciting and chanting *sutras* accompanied by music. The statues of Wen Chang, Tian Long, and Di Ya were exhibited. The three volumes of the *Da Dong Xian Jing* were recited and they prayed for a lucky year.

The gathering was held in the courtyard of one of the merchant's homes; the merchant provided tea and meals. Each year it was at a different home. The merchants' families came, listened, and enjoyed the hospitality. A barber, who had spare time, each day at closing time visited all twenty shops and collected five copper coins towards the expenditure of next year's gathering.

On the 15th day, the shops opened and there was a laboring tools fair in Da Yan.

On the 20th day, the Clan Mu held a ceremony for the Great Black General in Heaven at the Tibetan Buddhist lamasery in Bai Sha, a village north of Da Yan. A member of the Clan Mu rode a horse to Bai Sha. When he arrived at the lamasery, the lamas recited *sutras*. The head lama unlocked the door and the Clan Mu member threw a large, live, cock into the lamasery.

After this opening ceremony, everyone could enter the lamasery. *Joss* sticks were lit and people knelt down in front of the statue of the Great Black General in Heaven. He was a god with a black face, three heads, six arms; he guarded the front gate so that evil spirits could not enter. People prayed that the Great Black General in Heaven would bless them and protect them. The temple was only open to the public for this one day of prayer each year.

6. CONFUCIAN GATHERINGS

Around February 8th and August 29th, Confucian gatherings were organized and sponsored by the Lijiang County Education Bureau. The ceremony, a very old tradition, followed *Da Cheng Yue Zhang, Music Scores of Great Achievements,* a book distributed by the central Guomindang Government. *Dongjing* Society members were invited.

A long table was set up and on it was placed a wooden board with Confucius' name. At daybreak, as the cock crowed, the ceremony started; the main governor of Lijiang County, followed by four prominent officials and intellectuals, led all the invited participants in bowing down three times in front of the wooden board. Then, the *Dongjing* Society members recited the *sutra* book with musical accompaniment. After, there was a sacrifice of oxen, goats and pigs; animal dealers provided the money for the ox offering, butchers the pigs and goats. Pieces of paper were distributed to privileged people with their meat allotment; the governor received twelve *jin*, other officials eight or nine *jin*, He Ru Lin four or five *jin*; He Ru Lin was considered an important person. The gathering lasted about three hours.

As an adult, He Yi An participated in these gatherings at the invitation of the local government; they had no special meaning for him.

7. MARRIAGE

On the first day, He Ru Lin's and He Yi An's friends swept and cleaned their courtyard and four buildings. A colorful tent was set up and red lanterns hung in their courtyard. After completing the preparations, their friends were served a simple meal.

The wedding ceremony was on the second day. All guests offered the family congratulations and gifts, a plate of rice, brown sugar, and two silver dollars. To collect the bride, four sedans were used: one for the groom, one for the bride, one for the go-between, and one for the best woman. The wedding procession traveled to Yu Ji's house with the sound and excitement of Chinese trumpets, drums beating and firecrackers. When they arrived, the door was closed. The go-between knocked on the door several times until it was opened; once opened, the best woman entered and presented gifts of tea and cakes to Yu Ji's parents. Only wealthy families had a best woman; she represented the groom's parents in helping to accept the bride. She was from the groom's family and not a widow. He Yi An wore a long, blue gown and a black mandarin jacket. Yu Ji wore a long red coat and two pieces of red silk covering her head and her face.

The wedding procession returned to He Yi An's house with the sound of and excitement of Chinese trumpets, drums beating and firecrackers. According to Naxi tradition, the bride's parents did not attend the wedding ceremony nor the banquet at the groom's house. Their daughter was going to join the groom's family and was gone forever.

When the wedding party arrived at He Yi An's house, they entered the courtyard and walked into the corner which was decorated with hanging scrolls with pictures of gods in heaven. A Daoist priest performed a ceremony sacrificing to heaven and earth; his *sutras, Tui Che Ma, Farewell to Carts and Horses,* had three functions: first, to ask the sedan men to leave; second, to ask the bad spirits to leave who might have accompanied the couple back from the street into the house; third, to congratulate the couple and pray that they would live long and treat each other well. When the priest finished reciting, the couple knelt down once.

The wedding party then moved into the downstairs main room. On the wall, directly in front of them, hung a scroll with the Chinese character for happiness. In front of the scroll, there was a square table with a pair of red candles on it. On the floor in front of the square table, a small piece of red carpet was placed. He Yi An stood on the left with Yu Ji to his right; she still had the red silk covering her head so that nobody saw her face. The best woman stood beside her.

He Yi An first greeted the heaven with the Chinese hand salutation (placement of cupped left hand over right fist followed by a downward movement; a Chinese sign of respect and acknowledgment) and then knelt down on the red carpet; Yu Ji knelt down with the best woman's assistance. The couple then greeted the earth and He Yi An's ancestors in a similar fashion. The couple then turned to the left and knelt before He Ru Lin; they turned to the right and knelt before Qi Zhen.

One of He Yi An's friends gave his parents small glasses of liquor. He Ru Lin poured some liquor on the floor; their ancestors now knew about the young couple. He Ru Lin then made some congratulatory remarks to the couple wishing them long life and a good relationship. His parents drank the liquor. Some close relatives made similar remarks and drank some liquor. Then, He Yi An led Yu Ji upstairs to their wedding room. The best woman and other older female relatives, from both families, carried food and tea water to accept the bride and joined her in the wedding room where they sat together all that day. He Yi An returned to the courtyard to receive the guests.

A large banquet of six bowls and six dishes was served to the mainly male guests. Because males and females did not mix socially in public, it was the custom to invite them separately. The seating arrangement at the banquet was very important; at the first table, the first seat was for He Yi An's uncle, then older relatives according to their ages. A gong was sounded to signal the departure of each new dish and each new bowl from the kitchen; in the courtyard, musicians played a bamboo flute and *er hu,* a two-stringed fiddle, when a dish was served to each table and two Chinese trumpets when a bowl was served.

During the banquet, Yu Ji was sent a bowl of rice, a bowl of red meat, boiled pork, several other dishes, and a pair of red chopsticks. This symbolized a red letter day as Yu Ji was becoming a member of He Yi An's family. The best woman helped Yu Ji to eat her wedding meal. After the banquet, He Yi An's friends went upstairs to play jokes with Yu Ji attempting to pull off the two pieces of red silk from her face.

On the third day, older male and female relatives, as well as female friends and neighbors, were invited. The couple knelt down for close relatives and older people; they bowed to other guests. The guests were served a large banquet of six bowls and six dishes, with musical introduction.

On the fourth day, the couple went to Yu Ji's home for the day; her parents entertained their relatives, friends, and neighbors with a banquet. He Yi An's parents did not attend because He Ru Lin was not that famous nor wealthy and would have incurred the added expenditure of hiring two extra sedans.

8. FUR AND LEATHER SOCIETY GATHERINGS

In the Black Dragon Park, the Fur and Leather Society owned a two-story house. It was for rent all the year except March 5th through March 7th. Each year on these three days, the Society held a gathering in memory of the forefathers of their profession. Four families were in charge of the activities and hosted over one hundred persons, including bosses, masters, and apprentices from about thirty shops. When these families were selected, the previous year, each received one hundred silver dollars and they shared the annual rent from the Society's public farm lands, forty *mu* (approximately 6.5 acres) in Hong Wei.

During the gathering, four portraits were displayed and four large wooden boards set up. The names of Guan Xue Xian (the governor of Lijiang Prefecture in the Qing Dynasty), Bi Gan (the civil God of Wealth), Xuan Yuan (an ancient Emperor, the first person to use flax (burlap) to sew clothing), and Zhang (the master invited by Guan from Shan Xi province who originally taught the profession in Da Yan) were carved into the boards; the boards were exhibited in this order from left to right. On the first evening, for supper they were served only noodles, a symbol of longevity.

The second day was the main day of the gathering. The Society members congratulated those apprentices who had completed their four years of study. Their masters contributed one silver dollar per graduating apprentice. Each Society member paid a fifty-cent copper coin towards the expenses. The remainder of the expenditure was covered by the four host families. Each gathering cost about one hundred and twenty silver dollars. For lunch and supper, the members were served six bowls and six dishes.

On the third day of the gathering, each of the four host families returned the hundred silver dollars to the Society plus ten silver dollars as interest. Four new host families were selected for the following year's gathering and each received one hundred silver dollars. The leader of the Society presided over a general meeting at which members who had violated the Society's rules during the preceding year were punished. Those who produced sub-standard products and those who attempted to lure masters to their shops by higher salaries were either fined or suspended from doing business for a period of time.

9. SANDUO FESTIVAL

During February each year, the Naxi celebrated the Sanduo Festival in Bai Sha. Da Yan was divided into six *jia,* or administrative districts, organized on the basis of households. Yi Yong, Yi Zheng, Yi Shan, Yi He, and Yi Sheng were the six *jias.* He Yi An lived in Qi Wen which was one of the four villages in Yi Shun. Qi Wen had thirty-seven families. Each *jia* had a day assigned to celebrate the festival. It was the custom for the townspeople to stay overnight in several rooms near the temple. Villagers celebrated only during the day and returned home. The Sanduo Temple, Bei Yue, opened on February 3rd for people from the first *jia.*

Each year, He Ru Lin took He Yi An to Bai Sha to celebrate the Sanduo Festival. They traveled to Bai Sha on February 7th with a member of the Clan Mu. The large central temple doors were opened only for Clan Mu members; the common people entered through two smaller side doors. In the main temple, there was a special room for the Clan Mu. The member of the Clan Mu lit *joss* sticks, knelt down in front of the Sanduo statue, and prayed. His first prayer was for Sanduo to bless the Clan Mu with a good year; his second prayer was for Sanduo to bless the Naxi with a good harvest. After his prayers, he had his fortune told for the coming year. By reading three rolls of dice thrown in a large bowl, the temple keeper, a local wise man, told the fortune. The fortunes came from a Chinese book. Others then paid to have their fortunes told.

Two families who rented local land from the Clan Mu provided a pig and a goat as offerings. After the ceremony, the animals were sacrificed and the boiled meat served to all the people. A family from Yi Shun brought a pig as an offering for their *jia*. Common people brought a cock as an offering. During the evening, young people danced and men gambled.

On the morning of February 8th, the member of the Clan Mu entered the temple, lit *joss* sticks, knelt down in front of the Sanduo statue and made an offering of the pig and goat heads. After this offering, he had his fortune told for the second time. During the morning, others had their fortunes told. After lunch, they returned to Da Yan. He Yi An found this festival interesting and entertaining.

INSIGHTS

1. Rock published *Ancient Na-khi Kingdom* (Cambridge, Harvard University Press, 1947) and a series of articles in *National Geographic.*

2. London, John Murray, 1957.

3. Ibid., pp. 213–214.

4. It is a tradition to recite portions of the *sutra* book *Opening Prayer* of the *Da Dong Xian Jing,* the immortal Daoist verses.

5. A percussion instrument used in *Dongjing* and Buddhist music to add rhythm.

6. "Concentrate your mind" from the *sutra* book *Opening Prayer* contained in the *Da Dong Xian Jing.* All material in italics is from this Daoist bible.

7. Gift giving is a basic custom among Tibetans and a *hada,* "cloth that binds," or felicity scarf, is a symbolic gift of purity and respect.

8. All dates are according to the Chinese lunar calendar.

9. His adult name, He Yi An, is used throughout the text to avoid confusion with his other names.

10. Disgusted with the inefficiency and corruption of the Imperial government, despondent over China's economic subjugation by Western powers, and embarrassed by her second-class international status, Chinese "patriots" under

the auspices of Dr. Sun Yat-Sen, a Western educated reformer, overthrew the Qing Dynasty in 1911 and established the Republic of China. The governing party, which eventually was ruled over by Chiang Kai-Shek, was known as the Guomindang.

The downfall of the Manchu emperor marked the end of China's imperial history, which spanned some four thousand years. The establishment of the Republic of China marked a new epoch in the nation's history.

However, factions within the new Republic, motivated by the desire for personal power and gain, made for an unstable new government. Soon it was clear that some even planned to re-establish Imperial rule. Years of fighting followed, both military and legal. Autonomous warlords sprang up in the provinces and declared independence, and the major factions along the coastal regions split into north and south. Secret societies, fermenting with revolutionary zeal, threw their allegiances first one way and then another. Grand ideas for the renewal and Westernization of China were flung left and right, but due to a non-existent central government, very few were implemented.

As the other world powers moved toward and then through World War I, China struggled with her own internal conflicts. However, because of the world war, Western imperial and economic encroachment diminished, allowing China to begin to develop her own industries and economy.

Matching this civil unrest was intellectual upheaval. Younger Chinese, who had studied abroad, returned to their homeland and became dissatisfied with what they considered outdated and restrictive cultural traditions. Confucianism fell out of favor with young intellectuals, as did the centuries-old bureaucratic system of government exams. This dissatisfaction opened Chinese minds to the "modern" and "scientific" doctrines of Marxism, which would later flourish under the leadership of Mao Tse-Tung. In all, it was a time of drastic change.

There were major changes in Da Yan. Chinese became the official language; He Yi An spoke Chinese with his parents and Naxi with his grandmother. The new government organized a Chinese Language Society which Naxi men could attend to learn to speak Chinese. Members caught speaking Naxi were fined one copper coin. Men were forced to cut their pigtails. During a two week period shortly after the Republic was established, some revolutionary elements in Da Yan went to all the local temples and monasteries and tore down and smashed the statues. Clay statues of Wen Chang were destroyed.

At this time, some local citizens complained to the new governor that the *Dongjing* Society belonged to the older feudal times and should stop its activities and gatherings. The new governor was a member of one of the Kunming *Dongjing* Societies. To satisfy these local citizens, he suggested that the name be changed; from 1912, the Da Yan *Dongjing* Society was known as the Lijiang Music Society. However, the governor allowed them to continue their activities and gatherings. Since they continued to function as a *Dongjing* Society, this name is maintained.

11. A geomancer is one versed in divination by means of the figure made by a handful of earth thrown at random or by figures or lines formed by a number of dots made at random.

12. A one hundred cent silver coin was a silver dollar; copper coins ranged in value from one to fifty cents. Rice cost seven or eight copper coins per *jin*, a measure of five hundred grams.

13. There was no tuition fee but each student had to purchase his own textbooks. They studied for two four-month semesters: from the middle of February until the middle of June and from the middle of September until the middle of January. The remaining time was holidays. His class of thirty boys was taught by a Naxi. The teacher's salary was fifteen silver dollars per semester; it came from the Lijiang County Education Bureau and from the sale of grain from the Qi Wen public field. This was an average salary at the time.

The students were quite rowdy, speaking loudly and shoving each other. The teacher maintained discipline with the use a piece of wood to hit the palms of the delinquent students. For the most troublesome students, the teacher would ask them if they wanted to ride the red or black horse. The student lay on the colored bench and the teacher smacked his bottom; the black horse was the most severe ride. Students wanting to go to the toilet had to approach the teacher's desk, bow, and ask permission. If granted, the student collected a wooden board and went. Only two students were allowed out of the classroom at one time.

14. Each relative contributed one or two silver dollars towards the funeral expenses.

15. Each *sutra* is a poem or story about how well a person treats his or her parents. Together they form a Daoist book.

16. Higher primary school cost two silver dollars per semester. Each student purchased his own textbooks. Each semester, a teacher earned about twenty silver dollars from the Lijiang County Education Bureau.

17. The year was calculated from the *Ten Heavenly Stems* and the *Twelve Earthly Branches.* Five cycles of a Stem plus one cycle of an Earthly Branch.

18. The three worlds were Heaven, Earth, and Water.

19. The five gods were from east, south, west, north, and center.

20. School discipline was very strict. Each semester the tuition was three silver dollars with an additional eight silver dollars for the two meals per day. Teachers' salaries were graded according to the subject they taught. Chinese language, English, and mathematics teachers earned sixty silver dollars per semester, a good salary. Teachers of the other subjects earned less. For two exceptional teachers, of Chinese language and English, the school sent sedans to accept them and send them home.

21. Incantation of mind purification.

22. Five deities were heart, liver, spleen, lungs, and kidney. These are the "body parts" to which He Yi An refers. The practice of *qigong* is thought to regulate these organs.

23. Terrible desires were devils.

24. Each relative contributed two to three silver dollars towards the funeral expenses.

25. Relatives contributed thirty copper coins towards the funeral expenses; this was less than previous family funerals but the standard amount at this time.

26. *Prajnaparamita sutra*, the *Goddess of Mercy sutra*, an aid to crossing over from this shore of birth and death to the other shore.

27. Anti-Japanese War: (1931-45) Imperialist members of the Japanese military took control of the civilian government in Japan, and began a campaign to conquer China. A successful takeover of Manchuria in 1931 emboldened these militarists and encouraged them to plant footholds in North China. By 1938, the Japanese had captured major portions of coastal and central China. This phase of Japanese aggression brought to a halt the destructive civil war between the Nationalist and Communist factions.

United by the very real danger of being overwhelmed by the Japanese, the warring parties declared an ideological truce and combined their strengths to combat the foreign incursion. Chiang Kai-Shek was chosen to lead the combined forces. It was a conflict that would last almost a decade. The Guomindang resistance efforts, though at times woefully unsuccessful, were enough that Japan dedicated a significant portion of its military resources to the China campaign, resources that otherwise would have been directed against the Allies. After Japan's surrender in August, 1945, all Chinese lands were evacuated by Japanese forces.

28. Chinese Civil War: (1945 -1949) After the end of World War II and the Anti-Japanese War, China emerged as the major power in the Pacific. Chiang Kai-Shek enjoyed international prestige and the Chinese people experienced a renewal of national pride. However, both Chiang and the nation were exhausted from the extended struggle with Japan. With the removal of the threat of Japan, an old enemy emerged — Mao Tse-Tung and the Communists.

Mao had quietly consolidated and expanded his forces during the struggle with Japan. The Red Army was larger than ever, and his propaganda machine had been busily at work in the countryside, amassing peasant support and creating unrest.

Despite mediation attempts by the United States, the Guomindang and Communist forces turned on each other. Although initially successful, the protracted campaign soon went against Chiang Kai-Shek. On October 1, 1949, Mao declared the establishment of the People's Republic of China. Chiang Kai-Shek and his armies fled to Taiwan, and though the Guomindang leader declared the establishment of a government in exile, it was the end of the Nationalist regime on the mainland.

29. In 1950, a new currency was introduced with the *Renminbi yuan* (RMB ¥) replacing the silver dollar. Each *yuan* was worth one hundred *jiao*.

30. The Farmers' Associations were local police forces, comprised of farmers and cadres, which informed the people of central and local governments policies and regulated their implementation. In the Lijiang region, they were established in July, 1951. Because the activities of the Farmers' Association started to focus on urban administration it was renamed the Street Committee.

31. During this time, some of He Yi An's relatives helped them. His uncles were businessmen who had not owned any land. They were classified as landlords but all their possessions, including their clothing, were not confiscated. They passed on some of their old clothing to He Yi An and his family.

The same was true of Shang Yuan's elder brother and sister-in-law, who helped by providing used clothing for Lian Di and Qian Di. Since her brother and sister-in-law had been peddlers before liberation, they were classified as common citizens and lived in three furnished rooms in a large courtyard. They both worked at a weaving factory and their son trained to be a herbal doctor at the local hospital.

While teaching the *Dongjing sutras* and music in Jin Shan, a farmer had asked He Yi An to bless his only son; the boy grew up calling He Yi An 'daddy.' Learning of He Yi An's situation, the family sometimes brought them food.

32. During the peak time of the Great Leap Forward (Mao's plan to escalate industrial and economic growth) in 1957-58, the government wanted the people to live together, eat together. Feel communism. Initially, the public dining halls were free and open all day. Many people stopped working because free food was available everywhere all day. One year later, the government could not afford to feed everybody without payment, so food cards were issued by the Street Committees; all citizens had to eat in the public dining halls. No grain was sold in the market, only from government shops.

33. Anti-Rightist Movement: The severe curtailing of popular dissent and intellectual criticism of the government and its policies. Critics were relocated to camps for "corrective" ideological indoctrination.

34. Political study had started during the Land Reform on an intermittent basis. During the Cultural Revolution (1966-1976), almost every day there was political study; work during the day and political study during the evening. Frequent meetings for political study continued until 1983. After that time, political meetings were less frequent, but continued to be held.

35. Mao's book: Known as the "little red book," *Quotations from Chairman Mao* was a collection of proverbs gathered from

the leader's political writings and speeches.

36. In 1969, a boundary dispute led to a border incident in northeastern China with the Soviet Union. After this incident, the central government considered the Soviet Union its main enemy and feared an invasion. In response to this fear, it developed a strategic plan to distribute citizens from the cities to the countryside and major weapons and ammunition factories to isolated mountain areas. The central government also feared that in the event of a Soviet attack the four types of people might join with the enemy and stage an uprising against the Chinese Communist Party.

37. He Yi An believed farmers led miserable lives. Poor soil conditions gave them poor harvests and low incomes. Each day, they ate corn and beans; only on festivals could they afford rice. The women were quite poor and did not even have the Naxi leather skin capes.

    He suggested that if they raised goats, he could make capes for them from the goat leather. The village women were pleased that He Yi An made capes for them. The villagers arranged for an apprentice to study with him; later, there were two apprentices. The villagers often found ragged leather and asked him to mend their coats. People from Da Yan came to Ji Xiang and asked him to mend their coats. When they returned to Da Yan, he often gave them some eggs.

    The villagers had no idea how to solve problems. If somebody was sick and required medical attention, it was necessary to take a sum of money to the hospital. After the consultation, the patient received a form which he handed in at the office. After paying the charge, the form was stamped, and the person received the medicine from the pharmacy. The doctor's fee was included with the medicine.

Since the villagers were paid only once a year and bought items on credit at the village stores, they generally carried little money. Before the worried villagers would go around and borrow a little money from many different sources. He Yi An suggested that if the village head agreed to lend the sick person money, he could give him the full amount from his shop's earnings. In the countryside, it was possible to start a shop with the permission of the village head; the income went to the village. There were no taxes to pay as in Da Yan.

38. He Yi An's family was the last landlord's family to leave Da Yan for the countryside. Some landlord families stayed in the countryside for as little as two months, others as long as two years, before returning to their towns and cities. The government had lost interest in controlling them. The villagers complained about the insufficient food supply for both themselves and the outsiders as well as the educated town youths coming to live among them. The villagers made trouble. This situation made it relatively easy for families to return to their towns and cities. He Yi An's family was the last to return to Da Yan from the countryside.

39. After contracting with the Street Committee to run their shop, they incurred the following monthly expenses: ¥24 contract fee, ¥30 shop rent, ¥4 fee to the Administrative Bureau of Industry and Commerce, ¥10 business tax, and ¥10 utilities.

40. Five of the fourteen poems of *Qing He Lao Ren*.

41. Lucky days according to the Chinese lunar calendar.

42. Closing Prayer for a *Dongjing* Society Wen Chang gathering.

FAMILY TREE

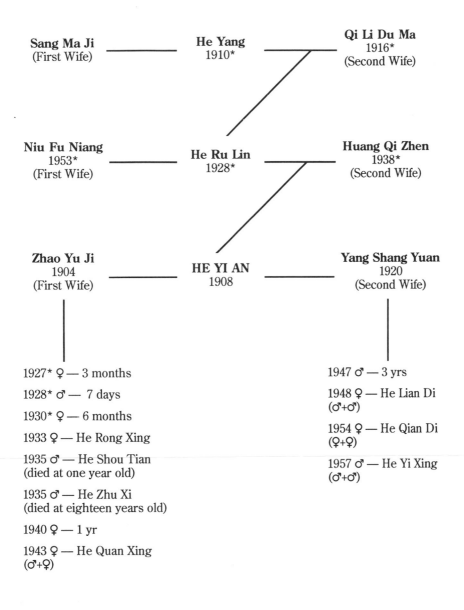

Sang Ma Ji
(First Wife)
———
He Yang
1910*
———
Qi Li Du Ma
1916*
(Second Wife)

Niu Fu Niang
1953*
(First Wife)
———
He Ru Lin
1928*
———
Huang Qi Zhen
1938*
(Second Wife)

Zhao Yu Ji
1904
(First Wife)
———
HE YI AN
1908
———
Yang Shang Yuan
1920
(Second Wife)

1927* ♀ — 3 months

1928* ♂ — 7 days

1930* ♀ — 6 months

1933 ♀ — He Rong Xing

1935 ♂ — He Shou Tian
(died at one year old)

1935 ♂ — He Zhu Xi
(died at eighteen years old)

1940 ♀ — 1 yr

1943 ♀ — He Quan Xing
(♂+♀)

1947 ♂ — 3 yrs

1948 ♀ — He Lian Di
(♂+♂)

1954 ♀ — He Qian Di
(♀+♀)

1957 ♂ — He Yi Xing
(♂+♂)

* year of death

Parentheses following children's
names indicate grandchildren.

■ EDITOR'S NOTE

Some insights were drawn from the following sources: *A Concise History of China,* Second Edition, by Milton W. Meyer, *The Rise of Modern China* by Immanuel C.Y. Hsu, *The Search for Modern China* by John D. Spence, and *Webster's 21st Century Concise Chronology of World History.*

■ A Note on English Spellings of Chinese Words

YMAA Publication Center uses the Pinyin romanization system of Chinese to English. Pinyin is standard in the People's Republic of China, and in several world organizations, including the United Nations. Pinyin is also used in contemporary scholarship and journalism. Pinyin, which was introduced in China in the 1950's, replaces the older Wade-Giles and Yale systems.

Some common conversions:

Pinyin	Wade-Giles
Naxi	Na-Shi
Qi	Chi
Qigong	Chi Kung
Qing	Ching
Dao	Tao
Guomindang	Kuomintang

For more complete conversion tables, please refer to the *People's Republic of China: Administrative Atlas*, the *Reform of the Chinese Written Language*, or a contemporary manual of style.

PRINTED IN CANADA